A Brief History of Wales

A BRIEF HISTORY OF WALES

Gerald Morgan

First impresssion: 2008
Revised edition: 2011

Copyright © Gerald Morgan & Y Lolfa 2008

ISBN: 9781847710185

Published, printed and bound in Wales by
Y Lolfa Cyf., Talybont, Ceredigion SY24 5HE
e-mail ylolfa@ylolfa.com
website www.ylolfa.com
tel (01970) 832 304
fax 832 782

This book is for
Tom, Ciaran, Llew, Ifan and Tudor

Dyma'ch hanes, fechgyn.

Contents

Foreword

I have been in love with the history of Wales since I was ten years old, when my father's two bibliophile brothers, Jack and Bill, gave me *A Short History of Wales* by O M Edwards and *Flamebearers of Welsh History* by Owen Rhoscomyl. The names of the great princes rang in my imagination. Later I was to discover that, because of family involvement in the Rebecca riots, my great-grandfather had been shot and badly wounded by an English policeman, and imprisoned for twelve months. It is a nice irony of history that that policeman, Captain Napier, was the founder of the Glamorgan Cricket Club, which I supported.

During the sixty years and more after those revelations burst on me I have tried to gain some small grasp of the complexities of history, and have tried to grasp the extraordinary changes which have taken place in Wales during my lifetime. I therefore appreciate the impossibility of the task which Lefi Gruffudd of Y Lolfa invited me to undertake. A history of Wales in twenty thousand words! But fools rush in… I would therefore like to thank Gwasg y Lolfa for commissioning this work, my editor Dafydd Saer, the Welsh Books Council, and Dr John Davies, historian of Wales, for his kind advice and encouragement. Thanks to the Welsh Assembly Government Press Office for the picture of the Senedd on p.139, and the Royal Commission on Ancient and Historical Monuments Wales for the picture of Tomen-y-Mur on p.11.

Gerald Morgan

1. Beginning to be Welsh

Julius Caesar, describing his brief raids on the Kent coast in 55 and 54 B.C., told his Roman readers that the interior of this mysterious island was inhabited by people who painted themselves blue, wore skins and lived on meat and milk. In fact the people of the west used cloth and grew corn for bread, as well as breeding cattle and sheep. That they painted themselves blue on special occasions is certainly possible, but Caesar was more interested in presenting the inhabitants of Britain to his readers as barbarians dependent on stock-rearing,

Tomen-y-Mur Roman fort Crown copyright RCAHMW.

in contrast to the civilised bread-eating Romans. Over a thousand years later Gerald of Wales, who actually knew better, was still repeating roughly the same story to entertain a sophisticated French-speaking audience. The moral: people have always believed myths about the Welsh, and the Welsh have believed myths about themselves.

In 43 A.D. the Romans returned, and within a few decades their ruthless military machine had overwhelmed the Celtic-speaking peoples of southern Britain. They threw a network of roads over their new province, linking military fortresses and civilian settlements. For three hundred years they exploited the island for its rich deposits of lead, and grew corn across the south and east in large quantities for export to Gaul. On a darker note, they exploited the islanders themselves, especially perhaps in the north and west. Unlucky Britons, both male and female, were taken as slaves; more fortunate men were recruited as soldiers to serve in Spain, Africa or Syria, while the luckiest became Roman citizens, speaking Latin, living in towns or country villas, their wives and daughters wearing their clothes and hair after Roman fashions.

What of the peninsula we call Wales? When the Romans came, there were indigenous tribes: warlike Silures in the south-east, peaceable Demetae in the south-west, Ordovices in the centre and north, Deceangli in the north-east, and perhaps Cornovii further south. Since the mountainous landscape of the north and west of Britain was less hospitable than the south, Roman civilisation did not penetrate it as thoroughly. The Welsh peninsula had only two tiny towns, Caerwent and Carmarthen, and a handful of villas along the south coast; elsewhere there were military forts. The native Celtic language – British – survived all across this highland zone.

Eventually, Christianity began to spread in the island, brought by merchants and their wives, by missionaries from Gaul and possibly by soldiers. By the fourth century raiders from north, east and west were attacking Britain's shores. By the fifth century Roman control had collapsed, replaced by the re-emergence of tribal chiefdoms. For several generations these chiefs used proud Latin titles to describe themselves, endowed Christian churches, and spoke a much-changed British language with many borrowed Latin words, especially words to do with building and commerce, slavery and punishment. They remembered the name of Cassivellaunus (Caswallon), the king who resisted Caesar; legends told of Caesar's defeat and of Magnus Maximus (Macsen), the British warrior who became emperor of Rome and who loved Helen of Segontium (Caernarfon), after whom roads were named.

The Welsh peninsula had no natural boundary separating it from the rest of the island. Its inhabitants

Magnus Maximus

were part of a British-speaking congeries of chiefdoms reaching from the Forth-Clyde line all the way to Land's End and across the sea to Armorica, which they colonised and named Brittany after themselves. They did not long control the south and east of the island, which from the fifth century came increasingly under the rule of Germanic-speaking settlers whom the British called *Saeson* – Saxons. The Saxons in their turn called the native inhabitants *Welsh*, meaning 'strangers', people who had come under Roman influence, though the Welsh themselves clung to the name of Britons. There were also settlements of Irish in the west.

In the absence of any British historians, various memories of this period were believed by posterity. The Irish were said to have been quelled by chieftains from northern Britain, Cunedda and his sons. It was thought of as a time of many wars against the Saxon settlers; sometimes the British were slaughtered or driven westwards, at other times they rallied under a charismatic leader – Ambrosius Aurelianus, Arthur, or Cadwallon, king of Gwynedd, who slew the king of Northumbria

> *Later people had other stories which formed their historical memory. They knew nothing of the ages of ice that had swept over northern Europe, but some features of the landscape caught their imaginations. Retreating sheets of ice had left huge banks of stones pointing south-westwards which were gradually covered by the rising Irish Sea. They have a remarkably artificial look about them, and it seemed they must have been built as ramparts against the ocean, until they had been overwhelmed and Cantre'r Gwaelod – the Lower Country – drowned. People saw that the huge megalithic tombs and hillforts visible in the landscape were not natural but artificial; many of the tombs were attributed to Arthur as his playthings, and the greatest of Welsh hillforts, Tre'r Ceiri, was named the Settlement of Giants.*

in 632 before being killed himself the following year. Today historians believe that the Saxon invaders were comparatively few in number but highly efficient in absorbing the native population.

It was certainly true that by the year 615 Saxon pressure had isolated the Welsh peninsula from the British of the north and the south-west. Memories of the northern British survived in Welsh poetry, which celebrated the names of King Urien and his son Owain, and the catastrophic defeat of the men of Gododdin (around Edinburgh) at Catraeth (Catterick). In the south, the arrival of the Saxons was seen as the result of treachery by a British king, Vortigern, execrated ever afterwards. Legend told of his flight to Gwynedd, where his attempts to build a fortification on the rock of Dinas Emrys foundered because of the subterranean battles of a white and a red dragon.

Vortigern is portrayed as weak, lustful and treacherous; he allied himself with the Saxons by marrying Hengist's daughter, Alis. Later Welsh writers would refer scornfully to the English as 'children of Alis'. Hengist destroyed the flower of the British chiefs by inviting them to a feast at which the Saxon hosts drew their long knives ('saxae') and slew their guests. This 'Treachery of the Long Knives' was to haunt later memories.

During the dark decades to which those bloody memories refer, something entirely different was happening in the Welsh peninsula: the native flowering of Christianity. It was nourished from a variety of roots: from a bishopric in what is now Herefordshire; from Caerwent; from contact with all the lands around the western ocean, and from Gaul. Men taught the message of Christ and celebrated his death and resurrection. They spoke British, but their source texts were the Latin gospels and liturgy, and a new layer of Latin loan-words appeared in the native language. Memorial stones were inscribed in Latin: *Here lies Catamanus, wisest and most renowned of kings; Here lies the body of Corbalengus the*

Ordovician. Particularly in the south-west of the Welsh peninsula, memorial inscriptions of single names survive in the Ogam alphabet, a form of writing invented in Ireland and used by Irish settlers. This was the period when the British language underwent a series of profound changes which gave birth to Welsh, Cornish and Breton.

Yet, if their texts were minimal, the memories these early Christians left behind were rich. We know hundreds of their names – many men, some women – connected with particular places. This was because they lived according to the monastic ideals, first developed in Egypt, which had spread across Europe: poverty, chastity, obedience. Their memory became attached to their little cells and to other places such as wells and rocks. Some became celebrated as teachers, like Teilo, some as charismatic leaders of communities, like Dewi (David) and Beuno. Their later followers founded new cells or churches and named them after their spiritual heroes. Women too, like Gwenfrewi (Winifred) and Melangell, became famous for their exemplary virtue.

These holy men and women had their problems. There were vivid memories of a native-born Briton who taught in Rome that orthodox ideas about original sin and salvation were wrong. The Pelagian heresy was named after him, and became current in Britain, where it took the combined efforts of Welsh saints and Ger-

Bardsey (Ynys Enlli), island of saints

manus (*Garmon*) of Gaul to stamp it out. Equally vivid was the memory of Augustine of Canterbury. In 603 he attempted to assert his authority over the bishops of Wales, who rejected his arrogant approach. Legends grew of conflict between saints and kings such as Arthur and Maelgwn. Many centuries later, the lives of some of the foremost saints – David, Cadog, Padarn, Brynach and others – were written, not as biographies, for the facts were lost, but as pious memories of miracle and folklore, and as claims for status and land.

Meanwhile, the early kingdoms of the Welsh peninsula become, in retrospect, more recognisable: Gwynedd in the north, Dyfed in the south-west, Powys in the east, Morgannwg and Gwent in the south-east. Gwynedd looked back to Maelgwn, reckoned to have died in 547, as a pivotal figure in its history. Powys treasured the memory of a time when it reached beyond what is now Shrewsbury, its heroes the sixth and seventh century figures of Llywarch the Old, Cynddylan and Heledd, treasured in plangent verse. Dyfed preserved in its name the memory of the Demetae and Gwent of the Roman markets, while Brycheiniog and Morgannwg claimed human eponyms, Irish Brychan and Morgan the Old. During the eighth century English settlers pressed into east Wales, building earthworks which were eventually subsumed by the colossal ditched bank named after Offa, king of Mercia (d. 796).

With the passing of the age of the saints and the establishment of the Welsh and English patterns of divided kingdoms, the Welsh peninsula passed into a period of partial isolation. In common with Ireland, the Welsh churches acknowledged practices which had become unacceptable or obsolete in the rest of the Western Church; a different way of deciding the date of Easter, a different mode of tonsuring priests. These Welsh churches formed a loose pattern of mother-churches and *clasau*, or monasteries. There were important centres of learning, especially St David's, Llanbadarn, Clynnog, Bangor, Llandeilo Fawr, Llantwit Major and Llancarfan. A fine illuminated manuscript of the Gospels, now at Lichfield, was kept at Llandeilo.

Part of Hywel the Good's Whitland memorial

The standard of Welsh learning is exemplified in the figure of Asser, who, in around 885 was invited to educate England's greatest king, Alfred.

Several of the many Welsh kings of the pre-Norman age stand out: Rhodri the Great (d. 877), king of Gwynedd, established the major royal line of Welsh kings which lasted, with interruptions, until 1283; Hywel the Good, king of Dyfed (d. 950), attended the English royal court frequently, visited Rome in 928 and was believed to have established a code of law for the whole of Wales, though the existing texts are much later; and Gruffudd ap Llywelyn (d. 1063), a ferocious warrior who briefly brought almost the whole of the peninsula under his rule, only for it to collapse at the hands of Harold Godwinsson. On occasion, Norsemen attacked Welsh coastal communities; they also established trading posts, certainly in Anglesey and probably in Pembroke, and gave place-names to coastal headlands and islands: Skomer, Skokholm, Bardsey, Anglesey, to name just a few.

How did the people of the Welsh peninsula identify themselves? That the word *Cymry* (meaning 'people of the same land') existed long before the coming of the Normans is clear, since part of north Britain still bears the name Cumbria. In around 930, an unknown poet appealed to the *Cymry* to join with others to destroy the English, but Hywel the Good was a friend to England's powerful king, Athelstan, and the appeal failed. The word Briton (*Brython*) continued to be used into the twelfth century, but *Cymro/Cymraes* was clearly usual by then, meaning a person who spoke Welsh.

Wales was a paradox. Its little kingdoms were fiercely independent, yet clearly subordinate to English kings like Edgar and Athelstan; indeed, six Welsh kings rowed Edgar on the Dee to show their subordination. All Welsh people spoke the same language, albeit with dialect forms. Poets used what was clearly a formal literary language recognised across the land, and storytellers travelled from community to community with stories and poems about Arthur, Myrddin (Merlin) and other heroes. Learned men developed the idea that the

British were the direct descendants of ancient Troy, just as the Romans had claimed for themselves. By tradition at least, there was one law for everyone, depending however on whether one was male or female, native or alien, married or unmarried, *bonheddig* or *taeog*. These last are difficult terms to translate: *bonheddig* meant of free descent, having a share in landownership; the *taeog* was a bondman, lacking any claim to land. How would this peninsula, with a common language and culture, but politically fragmented, cope with the most serious attack on it since the Roman legions?

Tourist authorities love to claim Welsh as the oldest living language in Europe, which is meaningless hype, but it certainly has a long history. Close to Breton and Cornish, a cousin of Irish, Scots Gaelic and Manx, Welsh has all the features of a Celtic language which delight linguists and baffle learners. Initial letters can mutate, so that for example cwch *(a boat) can become* gwch, chwch *and* nghwch *according to context. Prepositions are conjugated. There are no fixed words for 'yes' and 'no'. But don't be put off! It's far more phonetic than English or French. In its long life Welsh has borrowed words from Latin, Irish, Old English, Norse, French and English, but continues to coin its own vocabulary as well. Minority languages world-wide are in trouble, but Welsh is putting up fierce resistance.*

2. The Medieval Revolution

We can only imagine what effect the news of the 1066 battle near Hastings had in the princely courts of Wales. They were soon to feel its results: the united, powerful, cultured English kingdom had collapsed in an afternoon. How would the fragmented kingdoms of Wales survive?

King William quickly put several of his most ruthless followers in charge of the borderlands between English and Welsh. William, earl of Hereford, Roger, earl of

St David's Cathedral

Rhuddlan castle

Shrewsbury and Hugh, earl of Chester, began to chomp away at the Welsh kingdoms, tearing off the juiciest lowland areas and imposing timber castles, manors and even boroughs on them at Chepstow, Caerleon, Cardiff, Brecon and Rhuddlan, to name only the most important. They recognised rivers as territorial boundaries, though in mountainous Wales most boundaries followed watersheds, not watercourses.

In 1081, King William came on pilgrimage to St David's, recognising Rhys ap Tewdwr as king of Deheubarth in the south-west, which granted the Welsh some relief, but Gwynedd and Powys seemed doomed. In 1086, Robert of Rhuddlan paid William forty pounds for holding north Wales. With the killing of Rhys ap Tewdwr near Brecon in 1093 it seemed that all Wales

> *Sometimes the Welsh were lucky. When in 1098 their northern leaders were forced to flee their last redoubt on Anglesey, Magnus of Norway's fleet happened upon the Norman invaders and slew Hugh, earl of Shrewsbury. The Normans concluded that without control of the sea Gwynedd was too far to hold; the princes returned and reached accommodation with the Norman leaders. The north was saved.*

would be quickly swallowed up by England. What then made it possible for the divided Welsh, with their basic economy and limited military resources, to maintain the struggle for almost two hundred years more?

For a start, their divisions were also a strength. Welsh power could not be extinguished in one battle as England's had been. The Normans might overwhelm one lordship only to find themselves battling the next, and the next. Moreover, the great Norman barons had worries other than Wales; usually they held lands in England and France where they had to spend much time and wealth, and they owed service to their king. When the king was strong (William I, Henry I, Henry II, Edward I) the Welsh needed to tread softly, but when he was weak (William II, Stephen) the Welsh could take advantage. Two kings, John and Henry III, had periods of both strength and weakness, when the Welsh suffered or prospered accordingly.

Secondly, the Normans found the Welsh terrain difficult. Valleys and level coasts made advance easy, but the mountains and forests were another matter; the Welsh fought by hit-and-run tactics, not in formal battles. Advancing Norman forces lived off the land, but if the Welsh destroyed crops and withdrew with their animals to the hills, progress was difficult. Thirdly, the Welsh were willing to learn new skills. Fourthly, they were fortunate enough to produce several leaders of remarkable calibre, both military and administrative.

So Wales had two sets of rulers. Marcher (i.e. frontier) lordships stretched from Pembroke to Chepstow, and northwards via Brecon and Montgomery. Their lords were formidable men: the Clare, Braose and Marshall families gained frequent triumphs over Welsh princes. Within their lordships there developed divisions between Welshries and Englishries. Marcher lords tolerated Welsh law and exacted Welsh taxes in the former and applied their own version of Anglo-French law and taxation in the latter. Against them, Welsh princes and lesser lords held what was left: Gwynedd and Powys, a great tranche of the south-west (Deheubarth), the uplands of Glamorgan and small lordships in the east and south-east. Princes and Marcher lords alike acknowledged the king of England as their overlord.

The Normans brought about a series of revolutions in Wales. It was not only castles, manors and boroughs that were new to the Welsh. Within a generation the Normans were building in stone, both churches and castles. The Welsh learnt to build too, first mottes and ringworks, then stone castles and churches. They learnt how to besiege castles with ladders, catapults and under-mining. The Normans were great administrators; their kings may have been illiterate but they understood the importance of documentation and accounts, of having a chancery and exchequer. The Welsh princes too began to use these methods. They learnt diplomacy, how to compromise with the English crown, how to seek alliances in France and Scotland.

The Normans reformed the Church. They perceived an alien and outdated situation in Wales, so the country was divided into four dioceses with clear boundaries, each diocese into archdeaconries and each archdeaconry into parishes. Priests were forbidden to marry as they had been doing (not that the ban had much effect), and princes were told to put aside wives who were related to them by blood, even distantly (again the ban was inef-fectual). Normans were installed as bishops. Alongside major castles at Chepstow, Abergavenny, Cardigan, Brecon and others, Benedictine priories were established in subordination to English and French abbeys. Native Welsh monasteries, for example Bardsey, Beddgelert, Penmon, were either suppressed or reformed as priories.

Yet the Norman church reforms did not change

everything. The Benedictine priories remained small and Anglo-Norman in nature. Princes of Gwynedd rejected Norman episcopal appointees, while the Norman Bernard, bishop of St David's, took on Welsh ideals and campaigned for an archbishopric. Moreover, Normans realised that continuity of church dedications could be valuable (though not perhaps in cathedrals); the early Welsh saints were given *de facto* recognition, monks were encouraged to write their lives, and documents were assembled and copied to define the ownership of church lands.

More successful than the Benedictines were the Cistercian monks who reached Wales in 1131. By 1200 the Cistercians had thirteen monasteries in the country, many of them endowed by Welsh princes with great stretches of upland grazing and smaller lowland holdings. The monks and abbots were Welsh, and they supported the Welsh princes by serving as secretaries and ambassadors. The monks of Strata Florida kept a chronicle of annual events, and copied Welsh literary manuscripts. Strata Florida, Aberconwy and the rest were small compared with the major abbeys of England, but within Wales their influence was much greater than priories of other orders; moreover they were not under the control of Canterbury. Welsh families however did not favour monasticism for their daughters; there were only three Welsh nunneries.

Strata Florida abbey

There was often ferocious, treacherous and bloody conflict between Welsh and Normans, and with the English that the Normans became. Yet the same problems existed between and within the Welsh principalities. In pursuit of power, Welshmen murdered, blinded and castrated not only their Welsh enemies but their own relatives. Violent deaths were frequent. For example, of twenty-four men of the dynasty of Powys between 1075 and 1197, fourteen were killed or maimed. English kings and Marcher lords could be equally bloodthirsty and treacherous.

Welsh savagery is often blamed on the Welsh law of succession. Land ownership went by partible succession between sons or other males (in theory no woman could own land). It is often assumed that the same applied to lordship, and that the division of rule was necessary every time a ruler died. However it has been argued powerfully that this was *not* the case. The Welsh law-books list the king's heir as one of the court, and it seems clear that heirs were chosen, but that once their fathers died, jealous fraternal rivals often murdered them and then fell to squabbling. The Lord Rhys (d. 1197) had eight legitimate and seven illegitimate sons; the subsequent infighting broke up his kingdom of Deheubarth.

Nevertheless, matters slowly changed. Some Welshmen were willing to cooperate with the invaders from the beginning, either to gain their help against Welsh enemies or for personal gain. As the Welsh principalities demonstrated that they were not to be overthrown

Women were sometimes able to rise above the social and domestic roles to which they were bound. In 1109 the delectable Nest, mistress of Henry I, was willingly abducted by the rash Owain ap Cadwgan, prince of Powys. In 1136 Gwenllian, daughter of Gruffudd ap Cynan, died in battle at Kidwelly, leading her husband's army against the Normans. Senana, wife of Llywelyn the Great's illegitimate son Gruffudd, negotiated with the crown for her husband's release from the Tower of London.

Gerald of Wales was not the first to write about Wales in Latin for a European audience. In 1136 there appeared the History of the Kings of Britain *by Geoffrey of Monmouth. He purported to tell the history of Britain from the beginning, when refugees from Troy divided the land between Locrinus, Albanactus and Camber, the sons of Brutus. All these names had significance in Welsh (Locrinus = Lloegr [i.e. England], Albanactus = Alban [Scotland], Camber = Cymru [Wales], Brutus = Britain). The* History *tells of King Lear and his daughters, of Cymbeline and especially of Arthur's wars against the Saxons, and how the Welsh eventually acknowledged their loss of sovereignty over the island of Britain with the death at Rome of the last British king, Cadwaladr the Blessed. Despite the scorn of Gerald of Wales, Geoffrey's pseudo-historical work became the accepted history of Britain until the sixteenth century, a major propaganda influence in Welsh and English history, and was endlessly copied and translated. In particular the English version of the Arthurian legend took on Geoffrey's imperial Arthur rather than Arthur as conqueror of Saxons.*

quickly, Anglo-Norman lords were ready to intermarry with Welsh royal families; indeed on two occasions kings of England sent daughters (illegitimate, but recognised and richly supported) to marry Welsh princes. The cultural impact of such events must have been considerable. At multilingual courts the stories of the giant-killers Arthur, Cai, Bedwyr and Owain became known to the invaders and passed into French and thus European culture, much modified.

Intermarriage often, though not always, succeeded in creating peace and harmony. Gerald of Wales (d. 1223) was three-quarters Norman but grandson of the seductive Nest, daughter of Rhys ap Tewdwr. Not only did he write the two most entertaining books ever written about Wales, he maintained a long struggle to achieve Welsh church freedom from the domination of Canterbury, particularly in campaigning for his own appointment as (arch)bishop of St David's, ending in his own disillusion.

Against this background of huge cultural and political change, Welsh fortunes rose and fell. Gruffudd ap Cynan (d. 1137) had fought for several decades to ensure the recovery and re-formation of the kingdom of Gwynedd, enduring a decade in Chester prison before a dramatic escape. His son Owain Gwynedd expanded Gwynedd almost to the river Dee, effectively recovering the north-east from English rule, and in the south he helped Gruffudd ap Rhys of Deheubarth destroy the Normans near Cardigan in 1136. Later, Owain and his sons combined successfully with Gruffudd's son Rhys against Henry II in 1164. Both princes built and maintained castles, and at Cardigan in 1176 Rhys held a festival of music and poetry like those of southern France, seen in retrospect as the first eisteddfod. Rhys was, when not on the war-path, a man of wit and charm who eventually made a personal friend of Henry II, and was known as the Lord Rhys. South-east of Gwynedd, the principality of Powys survived in uneasy balance between the hammer of England and the anvil of Gwynedd; it fragmented in 1160.

After Owain Gwynedd's death in 1170 the power of Gwynedd weakened for thirty years, only to be revived by his grandson Llywelyn the Great. This remarkable man rebuilt and extended the power of Gwynedd through much of Wales, capturing Carmarthen, Cardigan and Montgomery, while King John was weakened by his rebellious barons, many of them Llywelyn's allies. Until his death in 1240, despite setbacks against the great Marshall family of Pembroke, Llywelyn was the most powerful ruler in Wales. He could rely on an able minister, Ednyfed Fychan, to whom was later attributed a coat of arms sporting three Englishmen's heads. Ednyfed's family was to endure longer in Welsh and English history than that of his prince.

The most remarkable example of marital diplomacy is the family of Llywelyn the Great. He himself had married Joan (Siwan), the strong-minded daughter of King John. When not bearing Llywelyn a son and four daughters she was able to act when necessary as a trusted ambassador to the court of England. The four daughters married Marcher lords, while the son, Dafydd, married Isabella de Braose even after Llywelyn had hanged her father William in 1230 for cuckolding him with Siwan. This event lived long in Welsh folklore.

All Llywelyn's successes collapsed with the failure of his childless son and sole heir Dafydd ap Llywelyn (d. 1246), who left the Welsh principality forfeit to Henry III. It remained for Llywelyn's grandson, Llywelyn ap Gruffudd, to make yet another bid to create a Welsh political and military entity. A great leader in war, he outmanoeuvred his brothers to rebuild and even extend the power of Gwynedd, making other Welsh lords his vassals. By 1267 he was able to pressurise the much-weakened Henry III to acknowledge him by treaty as Prince of Wales.

Yet Llywelyn faced appalling problems, some of his own making. His brother Dafydd was alternately ally and traitor, and Gruffudd ap Gwenwynwyn of Powys an implacable enemy. Llywelyn alienated Henry III's son Edward, the future king, by humiliating him in war. He tried to recruit the Welsh lords of the Glamorgan uplands to his cause, only to be frustrated by the powerful Gilbert de Clare, builder of Caerffili castle. He antagonised the bishops of Bangor and St Asaph. He taxed his people harshly to pay for new castles at Dolforwyn and Ewloe. He neglected to marry in time to

Llywelyn's memorial at Cilmeri

beget an heir, and stubbornly refused to pay to Edward I the homage or the money he had promised under treaty, fearing treachery.

Edward could not endure this contumacious presence for long. He had imperial ambitions, great resources and vast borrowing powers from Lombard bankers. He declared Llywelyn an outlaw in 1277 and with a three-pronged military attack, helped by the desertion to him of Llywelyn's vassals, quickly brought about Gwynedd's surrender. Llywelyn was left with an empty title, having control merely of Gwynedd west of the Conwy, comforted only by finally marrying a noble French bride, Eleanor de Montfort, at Edward's expense. Edward's builders began a chain of castles: Flint, Rhuddlan, Builth and Aberystwyth, which acted like a noose around Gwynedd.

The Welsh quickly learnt that Edward and his English officials could be even harsher than Llywelyn. When the prince's brother Dafydd rose in rebellion in Easter 1282, much of Wales joined the revolt, and Llywelyn placed himself at its head. Despite its early successes the revolt was doomed. Again Edward's armies moved ponderously west and north, trapping Llywelyn in Snowdonia, offering him only the prospect of living in England at the king's expense, demanding the total surrender of Gwynedd. The Welsh were defiant; such was the oppression of the English, they declared, that they would rather die than live, and that even if their prince surrendered, they would not. Llywelyn broke out of his retreat to rally the men of mid-Wales, only to meet with disaster and death at Cilmeri, near Builth, on 11 December 1282. His brother Dafydd was captured and savagely executed the following year.

At Rhuddlan in 1284 Edward announced his Statute of Wales. The lands of Gwynedd and Deheubarth would form the principalities of North and South Wales, while his loyal barons were amply rewarded with lands east of the Conwy and elsewhere. Thus Wales was now two lands – Principalities and Marcher lordships. Welsh land law would continue to function among Welsh people. Enormous and expensive castles were already being built at Harlech, Conwy and Caernarfon. The 1287 southern revolt of Rhys ap Maredudd was quickly stifled by a massive army. Madog ap Llywelyn's revolt in 1294 was far more widespread, bringing Edward's armies back yet again, and caused the building of Beaumaris castle, again at huge expense. Ironically, thousands of the king's paid soldiers in his four Welsh wars were themselves Welshmen, for despite their reputation for hot-headedness they were well-reputed warriors.

Wales had changed drastically since 1067. Numerous stone castles dotted the land, as did fine church buildings such as the cathedrals at St David's and Llandaff, the priories at Ewenni and Abergavenny and the Cistercian abbeys. There were attractive Welsh-built churches at Llanaber, Penmon and Aberffraw. Little boroughs existed in the shelter of castles established by the crown and by Marcher lords; villages grew as manorial centres. Trade developed, especially in livestock and wool. Despite immigrant pressure and the increased use of Latin, French and English, Welsh-language culture flourished, especially in the formation of prose tales (collected and eventually translated into English as the *Mabinogion*), in the translation of religious texts from Latin, and in the complex poetry addressed to the Welsh princes.

The greatest of these poems was Gruffydd ab yr Ynad Coch's elegy on Llywelyn ap Gruffudd. He saw that this was the catastrophic end of Welsh independence. The sea engulfs the land, the stars fall from the sky, Doomsday confronts us, why are we left alive when Llywelyn is slain, his head on an iron pole? Edward was given Llywelyn's gold circlet and his treasured relic, a fragment of the True Cross, for which later English

Caernarfon castle

kings built St George's Chapel, Windsor, with its ironic dedication.

Although Llywelyn's attempt to create a Welsh state ended in failure, the Welsh had their successes. Most notable was the development of Welsh self-consciousness. When at Pencader in 1163 Henry II demanded of a Welsh prophet to know the future, he was told that on the Day of Judgment no people other than the Welsh and no other language would answer for this part of the earth. Welsh law, the Welsh language, the myth of the Trojan descent, the memory of the historic struggle, all were still bonds connecting Welsh people as a recognisable nation – known variously as Cymru, Cambria, Wallia or Wales. However, that sense of nationhood, brought about in part by the continuous crushing pressure exerted from England, did not prevent regional loyalties within Wales from enduring to the present day.

Llywelyn ap Gruffudd

3. From Conquest to Union

With the deaths of Llywelyn and Dafydd, everything changed – and nothing changed. Their children disappeared into captivity. Folk memories of Llywelyn survived long in the Builth area; the local people were known for centuries as the Traitors of Builth, and they themselves told stories of Llywelyn's last hours, and of his (fictitious) betrayal by a blacksmith. Meanwhile, herding, ploughing and harvest, childbirth and burials, taxation and poverty continued as before.

While poets and the Welsh chronicler grieved ('all Wales was cast down'), after 1295 peace ensued for over a century, longer than Wales had ever known, with only brief interruptions. Nevertheless, the English boroughs quaked at the thought of Welsh insurrection and demanded protection and privileges for themselves and oppression for the Welsh 'snake in the grass' – Edward's phrase. With a few exceptions, the Welsh became second-class subjects in their own land. Edward, having fastened his royal yoke on the Principalities of North and South, rejoiced in this great step towards his recreation of an Arthurian empire like that imagined by Geoffrey of Monmouth, by holding a Round Table tournament at Nefyn in 1284. His gargantuan castle-building projects, with their dependent boroughs, forced the relocation of whole Welsh communities for the benefit of his colonial settlers. But at least he grasped that the Welsh needed a focus of loyalty, and though he taxed, he gave employment to Welshmen, especially as soldiers. Indeed, like other poor and mountainous countries, Wales produced more young men than its land could readily provide for.

In 1301 Edward revived the title of Prince of Wales, granted to Llywelyn in 1267, for his son Edward, thus giving him a title and lands, and perpetuating the only Welsh element in the British constitution until the Government of Wales Act of 1998. The title was an odd one, since there were long periods when no male heir existed (e.g. from 1547 to 1603, and from 1660 to 1714), and for Wales after the Acts of Union it became meaningless. But young Edward made something of a success of the position, recruiting Welsh knights, esquires and minstrels.

Edward I died in 1307, and Edward II failed to live up to his father's measure. He preferred entertainment to war and the company of his favourites to his queen. He lost Scotland to Robert the Bruce, and there were serious famines. Disaffection was widespread in England, and showed itself in Wales when Llywelyn Bren, the cultured lord of Senghennydd, driven by the sufferings of his people, besieged Caerffili castle in 1316, only to fail and be treacherously executed by the

Clearly Wales, both the Principality and the Marcher lordships, was now merely an appendix to England in military and political terms. Culturally however Wales was still its own country, and its greatest poet was composing at this time. We do not know Dafydd ap Gwilym's vital dates, but clearly he lived before 1350. He was of good family, not dependent on patronage as were his contemporaries. He preferred to delight in the month of May, in the power of the wind, in the song of the thrush, and in lovely women, who often spurned his wooing with mockery. There is a Chaucerian zest in his work, especially when joking at his own expense.

vile Hugh Despenser, a royal favourite. Widely loathed, Edward fled to Glamorgan, now a Despenser lordship, hoping for Welsh support, but the Welsh would do nothing to help. The king was captured near Neath, deposed and murdered.

In 1348 something far more terrible than Welsh insurrection happened – the Black Death arrived. A third of the population, perhaps 100,000, perished wretchedly. Though the plague retreated during the following years, it returned in 1361, 1369, 1379 and 1391. Surviving labourers escaped bondage, tenancies fell vacant, taxes went unpaid. The authorities attempted to clamp down on the inevitable rise in wages, but largely failed. The system of landowning by bonds of kinship was weakened, the Church enfeebled. The horrific disease had accelerated change.

Through these troubles one group of men remained true to the memory of royal Wales. Welsh poets hoped for the coming of a 'Son of Prophecy' to re-establish Welsh rule. Their candidate was the last heir in the main line of the princes of Gwynedd, Owain ap Thomas, known as Owain of the Red Hand, great-nephew to Llywelyn ap Gruffudd. Owain was a warrior, a mercenary captain known and feared across mainland Europe. He knew no Welsh, but he knew his descent, and had the backing of the king of France to claim his principality. As an evident threat to England, he was assassinated by an English spy at Mortagne-sur-mer in 1378. He is commemorated there, and in popular memory in south Wales, where Owain Lawgoch ('of the red hand') sleeps in a cave, awaiting the call to save his nation.

Another Son of Prophecy emerged at the turn of the century. Owain Glyndŵr must have seemed an unlikely candidate to lead a great rebellion. In 1400 he was middle-aged, with a brood of children. He owned estates at Glyndyfrdwy near Llangollen and Sycharth on the English border, the latter highly praised for its comforts by the poet Iolo Goch. He was well-educated, had spent time at the king's court and ridden with the king's armies twice in Scotland. Yet this man led a ferocious

Owain Glyndŵr

revolt which shook the land for a decade. Why? The poets recognised Glyndŵr because he was a direct descendant of the princes of Powys and Deheubarth and had connections with Gwynedd. As such, he was the one man to whom the disaffected and embittered Welsh could turn for leadership.

Proclaimed Prince of Wales, Glyndŵr seized Ruthin on 16 September 1400, while his Tudor cousins, descendants of Ednyfed Fychan, captured Conwy castle. In 1401 he reappeared at Hyddgen, on the slopes of Pumlumon, and the Welsh elements of the army sent against him changed sides. There was panic in England; parliament passed savage discriminatory laws against the Welsh. But Glyndŵr campaigned so successfully that he could ally himself with English rebels against the usurper Henry IV, with the promise of ruling a Wales extending to Worcester! The rebels failed, but Glyndŵr swept across Wales, capturing Harlech and Aberystwyth castles and burning his way down the Tywi valley and into Gwent. He assembled talented ministers,

Owain Glyndŵr's senate building in Machnylleth

concluded an alliance with France and proclaimed a policy for Wales's sovereign future, with universities and a Church independent of Canterbury.

> *Before and after Glyndŵr, Welsh-language culture continued to thrive. The poets were patronised by the* uchelwyr, *the country's gentry. They sang eulogies and elegies to these men and their wives, and to the Cistercian abbots – even to Edward III – and kept their genealogies. They also mourned their own children, celebrated their lovers, and disputed with each other. Their names ring to this day in the ear of a literate Welsh person: Guto'r Glyn, Lewys Glyn Cothi, Tudur Aled, Dafydd Nanmor...*

It could not last. Ironically, there were now two Princes of Wales, Glyndŵr and Henry of Monmouth. The teenaged Henry was a talented leader with massive resources. Glyndŵr's control shrank yearly until by 1411 he was a fugitive with a price on his head, followed by an offer of pardon which he ignored. Finally, he ensured immortality by vanishing, leaving behind the belief that he too slept in a cave, awaiting his people's call. He also left behind the ideal of a Welsh nation deserving of dignity. Succeeding generations rejected his actions but admired his courage; he remains *the* national hero, his qualities celebrated by Shakespeare.

Yet again the Welsh had to pick up the pieces. Few of the rebels were executed; some joined Henry V's army to fight at Agincourt, others resumed their lives as landowners and bardic patrons. Taxes had gone unpaid for years. Families and communities had been divided against each other, the rural economy had suffered.

Glyndŵr's seal

Yet life went on. Despite the long-lived antagonism of Welsh and English, they married each other. Families with English names and Welsh sympathies were known before and after Glyndŵr, whose wife was a Hanmer. While Wales lay exhausted, England became convulsed by the Wars of the Roses, the bloody struggle for the throne between the descendants of Edward III. In this murderous royal nest of England there was a Welsh cuckoo.

This was Owen Tudor of Penmynydd, descendant of Ednyfed Fychan, whose bold nerve and handsome figure took him to the bed of Katherine, queen mother of England (d. 1437), who bore him two sons, Edmund and Jasper. Edmund died soon after his marriage to Margaret Beaufort, great-great-great-granddaughter of Edward III, tainted by illegitimacy, but left a baby son, Henry Tudor (b. 1457), who by that tenuous claim was the only Lancastrian heir to the throne. To the Welsh poets therefore he was another Son of Prophecy. At the age of 14 he was taken by his uncle Jasper from Wales to Brittany to save him for his destiny.

In 1485, aided by the king of France, Henry brought a rag-tag army of English exiles and French mercenaries

Henry made all the right symbolic gestures to his loyal Welsh followers. He christened his first son Arthur, he assumed the red dragon on the royal coat of arms, he distributed offices to Welshmen and a certain amount of largesse to Welsh minstrels. But he was no fool; he was king of England and intended to remain so. Once seen as the first modern sovereign, he may be better viewed as the last of the medieval kings.

to Milford Haven and marched them north-eastwards, reaching England with their forces much increased by Welshmen. Under the flag of the red dragon his army destroyed the Yorkist Richard III and Henry was crowned on the battlefield of Bosworth. For the Welsh, the prophecy had at last come true: a Welshman ruled. Henry swiftly married Elizabeth of York, who, with her mother, actually had the best right to the throne, and was coincidentally a descendant of Llywelyn the Great.

Wales remained an anomaly, its principality separated from England by the Marcher lordships. In 1471 Edward IV had given his young Prince of Wales a Council at Ludlow to manage his estates, with wide responsibilities in the Principality, the March and the adjacent English counties; this experiment was continued by Henry VII. The lordships were closely supervised, and a growing number of them passed into the hands of the crown and therefore of the Council. The Council however was only effective when the king showed interest, and the English shires jibbed at being lumped in with the Welsh. Henry answered the appeal of many Welshmen for equal status at law with English-men by selling charters to them.

Henry arranged a fine marriage for Arthur, Prince of Wales, but barely was he married than he died in 1502. Catherine, his widow, who had brought a valuable dowry, stayed in England, and on the king's death in

1509 his surviving son, now Henry VIII, immediately married her. For twenty-five years he paid little attention to Wales. Crisis arose with his need for a male heir, which Catherine had not produced. Henry needed a new wife, but Catherine was aunt to Charles of Spain, Holy Roman Emperor, to whom the Pope was bound to listen, and an annulment was impossible. Therefore Henry threw off papal authority, proclaiming himself Head of the Church in England, and took a new wife. At the same time orthodox Catholicism was being challenged by reformers who protested against ecclesiastical corruption, and who sought to read the Bible in their vernacular languages.

The situation would affect Wales profoundly. Henry was faced with the wrath of Catholic Europe, and needed to secure his kingdom against invasion. The king needed to bind Wales closer to England. After all, had not his father invaded the island via Wales and seized the crown? Had not Glyndŵr's French allies

> *Modern dispute arose over the Act of 1536 and the status of the Welsh language. The only direct reference to it in the legislation simply says that no man could hold legal office without knowing English. To this some have added the reference to 'a speech nothing like, nor consonant to the natural Mother Tongue used within [England]'; certainly sardonic, the phrase refers to the*

fact of linguistic division without directly condemning it. The Act also refers to 'sinister usages and customs', but this quite clearly refers in context only to legal custom and practice. The Acts were not a direct assault on the Welsh language; they should be compared with Henry's legislation for Ireland, which fiercely condemned the Irish language.

Not that the Welsh language was secure. Even before 1283 English and French were penetrating Welsh life. The final abolition of Welsh law by the Act of 1536 certainly removed it from one of its few public domains; making wills and drawing up deeds of land were being done in English long before 1536. There were still great poets: William Llŷn (d. 1580), Siôn Tudur (d. 1602) and Edmwnd Prys (d. 1623). But clearly the bardic culture was dying for lack of change. There were eisteddfodau at Caerwys in 1523 and 1567, but no more.

Even more drastic was the anglicisation of the gentry. A Welsh gentleman learnt English; he might well marry an English woman; if the children knew Welsh it was sometimes from their wet-nurses rather than their parents. Welsh gentry began to abandon the 'ap' nomenclature in favour of English-style surnames. Sir John Salusbury of Lleweni (d. 1612) patronised Welsh poets, but he himself wrote verse in English. The Act of 1536 may be blamed in distant retrospect for accelerating these changes, but not for initiating them.

invaded in 1405? Moreover, legal reform would help to end the chronic lawlessness of the country, where brigands could escape from one lordship to another and laugh at pursuit.

A flurry of bills went through Parliament to do with Wales, dealing with trade and security. In 1535 Wales was subjected to the creation of Justices of the Peace, followed in 1536 by an 'act for laws and justice to be ministered in Wales in like form as it is in this realm [of England]'. This and its successor act of 1543 were, centuries later, termed the Acts of Union, though a better term would be 'assimilation'.

Endless modern ink has been spilt over the Acts of Union, or rather over one aspect of them which passed unnoticed at the time (see the previous box). Contemporaries however were entirely in favour. Welshmen gained access to an array of important positions, especially as Members of Parliament and JPs. The March was abolished; some lordships were incorporated into Shropshire, others went to make the pattern of thirteen counties so familiar for centuries. Thus Wales acquired the boundary which has remained virtually unaltered until the present day, though a difficulty arose over Monmouthshire. For the administration of justice, Wales was divided into four circuits of three counties each, and the 'spare' county (Monmouthshire) was attached to the English circuits, leading to the unnecessary legal formula 'Wales and Monmouthshire'.

Henry was anxious not only to control the Church, but to plunder it to meet his debts. First the bishops and clergy were pillaged, then between 1536 and 1539 all the Welsh houses of religion were 'persuaded' to surrender themselves, their inhabitants to be pensioned off and their lands confiscated by the crown. Suddenly there was a huge change of landownership, because Henry needed cash and began selling. Favourites and those with an eye to the main chance reaped the rewards. Sir John Price of Brecon, publisher of the first book in Welsh in 1546, took the priory there. The Devereux family acquired most of Strata Florida and the Stedmans the rest, the Mansels took Margam, the Carnes Ewenni, the Bradshaws St Dogmaels and the Barlows Slebech. And so on across Wales.

Nor was that the end. Henry had favoured Catholicism without the Pope; the young Edward VI and his advisers wanted out-and-out Protestantism. Relics were seized, stripped of their jewels and burnt. Thus perished Llywelyn's *Croes Naid*, Our Lady of the Taper at Cardigan, the image of Derfel Gadarn and many more. Pilgrimages, which had become hugely popular, bringing a steady income which had for example enabled St David's cathedral to become a splendid building, suddenly ceased. The careful parishioners of Llanrhaeadr Dyffryn Clwyd, who had recently erected a splendid stained glass East window, took it down and it was kept hidden for centuries. But an estimated 98% of church treasures were seized, glass and sculptures smashed, chalices and screens destroyed, altars broken, paintings whitewashed. There were pained murmurings by poets, but the Welsh gentry were too loyal to the Tudors to revolt as did Cornwall and the north of England.

Worse even than the vandalism, services were to be in English, less familiar to most Welsh believers than the original Latin. But there was a remedy. William Salcsbury, Protestant and humanist, published the liturgical readings, *Kynnifer Llith a Bann* in 1551 – the first printed Welsh translations of the Bible. He had published other Welsh books, and was ready for more, but

Treasures survive here and there: the Dolgellau chalice in the National Museum; the Mostyn Christ at Bangor; the great Jesse at Abergavenny; stained glass at a number of northern churches; screens like those at Llanrwst, Llananno, Llanegryn and others, and the restored shrine at Pennant Melangell. Great churches had been built before the Reformation at Wrexham, Hawarden, Gresford, Mold, Abergavenny, Chepstow, Beaumaris, Cardiff... but the loveliest churches are those hidden in the countryside: Partrishow, Llaneilian, Llanrhychwyn, Llantwit Major, Penmon, Llanwenog. Another casualty of the Reformation was church music, in which several Welsh composers excelled.

in 1553 Edward died, and Mary I crashed the vehicle of state religion into Catholic reverse. The vast majority of the Welsh may have been relieved; there were only three Protestants burnt in Wales compared with hundreds in England.

Elizabeth's accession in 1558 ended the Catholic reaction, though there was long-lived resistance. In 1563 an Act of Parliament called for the Bible and Book of Common Prayer to be translated into Welsh within four years. This was too much to ask, but in 1568 the Prayerbook and the New Testament appeared, translated by William Salesbury, helped by bishop Richard Davies. Complaints about Salesbury's pedantic spellings and style vanished in the wake of Bishop William Morgan's magnificent translation of the whole Bible in 1588. Hitherto, poetry had been the main expression of Welsh literary endeavour; Morgan created a new prose style of resonant dignity which gave the language a form

Bishop Davies's particular contribution was to the mythical history of Wales. Anxious to justify the Reformation, he argued in his preface to the New Testament that Christianity had been brought to Britain by Joseph of Arimathea and preserved in its pristine state until forcibly corrupted by the English. Protestantism was a return to authentic British – therefore Welsh – Christianity. Good propaganda – bad history.

and feeling which lasted into the twentieth century, as the King James Bible had done for English. Unlike the other Celtic languages, Welsh was given the chance to thrive, and despite the country's poverty, the huge cost of books, its diminished legal status, and the snobbery of many of the gentry, it did so mainly thanks to its position as an acknowledged language of worship and spirituality.

The title page of William Morgan's Welsh Bible

Wales after the Acts of Union

4. Protestantism, Gentry and Civil War

It was as well that the Welsh language thrived, because the Welsh had little else to distinguish themselves as a people except their name, their memories and their land. Even the landscape, nowadays iconic, was considered nothing special; rugged landscapes were thought barbarous, so by implication were those of its inhabitants who were insufficiently anglicised to please English taste. While Scotland was still a monarchy with all the necessary institutions of government, Wales only had its own language, and a history it couldn't quite forget. Many people tried to forget both. Institutional life had been completely absorbed into England. While there was now a recognisable boundary between English counties and Welsh counties, in political terms it was not a boundary at all. The Welsh had abandoned the national struggle in favour of English freedoms; the future struggle would be for identity. In 1746 the Wales and Berwick Act of Parliament laid down that they were included in England for legislative purposes. For Wales, see England.

With Henry VII's arrival in London, Wales had

acquired a capital city, and the Welsh flocked eastward. By 1600 there were more Welsh people in London than in any Welsh town. They were merchants, soldiers, mariners and pirates. They were lawyers and mathematicians, mapmakers, goldsmiths and clergymen, providing a dean of Westminster and bishops of Rochester and London, and later an archbishop of York, not to mention Elizabeth's chief gentlewoman, Blanche Parry and the comptroller of her household, Sir Thomas Parry. The names of Devereux, Perrot and Williams, and above all the earls of Pembroke, were well-favoured at Elizabeth's court. Men of the second and third generation wave of Welsh immigrants to England provided Elizabeth and James with their chief ministers, the Cecils, and the English language with two of its finest poets, John Donne and George Herbert, while another major poet, Henry Vaughan, was a Welsh-speaking physician living in the Usk valley. Another descendant of a Welsh migrant family was Oliver Cromwell.

Meanwhile, Welsh mythology influenced English history yet again. The imperial exploits of Arthur and the rumours, propagated by Dr John Dee (d. 1608), a London-born Welshman, that Madog ab Owain Gwynedd had discovered America in 1170, gave acceptable warrant for the expansion of British (Dee's word) overseas power. The idea blossomed with the beginning of conflict with Spain; in 1584 Hakluyt claimed Welsh authority for the tale of Madog, giving Elizabeth claim to the whole western seaboard of America. This eventually created the legend of Welsh Indians.

Shakespeare created two significant Welsh characters. Owen Glendower is of the past; at once gentleman-rebel and magician. Fluellyn epitomises the Elizabethan Welshman seen through English eyes, perceiving himself in essence as both Welsh and English, celebrating St David's Day, loyal to Welsh identity and the leek but super-loyal to the English crown, patronised and laughed at but not scorned, more than able to hold his own in badinage.

It is hardly surprising that the talented Welsh moved to England, since Welsh educational resources were feeble. True, small grammar schools were endowed at Abergavenny, Carmarthen, Brecon, Presteigne, Bangor, Ruthin and Beaumaris, and later at Haverfordwest and Cowbridge, but leading gentry families preferred English boarding schools. Oxford (especially after the foundation of Jesus College in 1571), the Inns of Court, and to a lesser extent Cambridge, provided opportunities for higher education. Girls of wealthy families had to be content with home tuition so that they could read, write, sew and manage households.

The Welsh landed gentry, reinvented by the Acts of the 1530s, were the backbone of loyal government in unified Wales for the next four and a half centuries.

These were men who exploited a whole battery of means to get and increase their estates, a process made easier by the Acts of Union. Best was to inherit land, otherwise an ambitious man could buy land, or failing that he could lend money at mortgage to failing farmers, then foreclose. He could marry money or an heiress. A good genealogy was more important in Wales than in England, but failing a genuine one, help could be obtained to fake one. Titles were useful adjuncts, but expensive to buy. Enclosure, gambling and theft were other ways of increasing one's estate.

The heads of the largest estates were well-placed for the highest positions in their counties: membership of parliament, deputy lieutenant, member of the Council for Wales. Lesser gentry sought the office of justice of the peace and rotated the annual county sheriffdom among themselves. All the threads of power lay in their hands; through the quarterly sessions of the peace they *were* local government, not only punishing petty crime but responsible for roads and bridges, oversight of poor law administration, and an ever-growing number of other tasks laid on them by parliament. Marriage and begetting children were fundamental; daughters of great houses who were not heiresses often had to 'marry down' into a lower rank of the gentry. For the gentry graded themselves according to their wealth, history and offices; there were parish gentry, county gentry and leviathans.

In 1584 the Historie of Cambria *was published. This remarkable volume presents a description of Wales, a translation of the medieval* Chronicle of the Princes, *with additional documents from the state archives describing the last negotiations between the Welsh of Gwynedd and the crown in 1282. There is a brief summary of the English Princes of Wales, including two pages on Glyndŵr's revolt. Re-worked by William Wynne in 1697 and by William Warrington in 1786, this was the serious written history of Wales up until the nineteenth century.*

Raglan, the last great Welsh castle

Wales was short of leviathans, though in north Wales there was the earl of Leicester, in the south the Somerset earls of Worcester at Raglan, the Herbert earls of Pembroke and the Devereux earls of Essex. All had bigger fish to fry in England. Every county or small group of counties had its families of upper gentry: Morgans of Monmouthshire, Carnes, Stradlings and Mansels of Glamorgan, Vaughans of Carmarthenshire, Breconshire and Merionethshire (where the Owens and Nanneys also flourished), Perrots of Pembrokeshire, Pryses of Cardiganshire, Wynns of Caernarfonshire, Bulkeleys of Anglesey, Mostyns, Thelwells, Middletons and Cloughs of Denbighshire and Flintshire, Herberts of Montgomeryshire. These families were frequently in fierce dispute with their neighbours, indeed within their own clans.

A major source of wealth for many of these great families lay underground. The Vaughans, Pryses and Powells between them owned most of Cardiganshire's sources of lead and silver. They were too dignified to take on the task of mining themselves, instead they used the Myddletons and other dynamic individuals like Thomas Bushell and Sir Humphrey Mackworth, contenting themselves with royalties while others took the frequent losses and massive profits. Metal extraction and woolworking represented the slow beginnings of the Industrial Revolution in Wales.

Many of the heads of these great families cannot have been nice men to know. The doctrine of *noblesse oblige* was as yet little known in Wales. Welsh gentlemen in Elizabethan and early Stuart times swaggered through the streets of little Welsh towns with gangs of thuggish liveried servants, bullying and fighting. Any perceived affront to their honour brought forth swords and cudgels. Elections, whether of MPs or bailiffs, could provoke riots if a particular gentleman or his candidate was snubbed. At election time, families often compromised with each other to avoid strife, but there were serious disturbances in a number of Elizabethan elections, and skulduggery was rife. At their worst the Elizabethan Welsh gentry were ruthless bullies, at their

In Wales the slow growth of popular Protestantism was helped by the publication in 1630 of Y Beibl Bach, *the little Bible; five thousand copies were financed by two wealthy London Welsh businessmen. The cause was even more successfully advanced by the popular verses of Rhys Prichard, vicar of Llandovery (d. 1644), whose work was memorised by thousands of the literate and illiterate alike, inculcating Christ's teaching and general morality, good habits and manners, and how to choose a wife.*

best they supported enterprise and learning, even to the point of writing valuable books of family and local history. Family life for their womenfolk was often a trial, sometimes a torment.

The gentry were expected to set an example of church attendance. Many of them were of families which had benefitted from Henry VIII's plunder of the church, and their religion was, to say the least, superficial. Others faced serious difficulties reconciling their loyalty to Rome with loyalty to the crown. Wales had its share of Catholic martyrs during and after Elizabeth's reign. Fear of Spanish influence and the Pope's desire to see the queen assassinated drove the government to persecute Catholics vigorously.

Welsh Catholics took all kinds of evasive action. Some left for Italy or France permanently, others left only to return. Some gentry families paid the fines, others compromised. Catholic books were published in France and Italy; a Catholic text was secretly printed in a cave near Llandudno in 1585. Most remarkable of the martyrs were the poet Richard Gwyn (d. 1584), William Davies (d. 1593) and John Roberts of Trawsfynydd (d. 1610). At the other extreme was the martyrdom of the Puritan John Penry (d. 1593), condemned as a traitor for his criticisms of crown and church, which included appeals for better provision for Wales. All these sacrifices were in vain; Elizabeth's version of Protestantism ruled, and the great majority conformed, though still nursing superstitious traditions such as belief in the *dyn hysbys* (cunning man) and the *toili* (phantom funeral).

Grinding poverty was the destiny of half the population, their homes vile hovels, their food poor, their work – if they had work – never-ending. Monastic charity had vanished, while giving by the rich to the poor decreased markedly, largely disappearing from Protestant wills. Public efforts were nevertheless made; at Swansea clothes and food were distributed, the price of corn kept down and orphan children were apprenticed, all of which must have happened in other towns where no records survive. But beggars, paupers, widows and pregnant single women faced a grim lot.

Between the extremes of wealth and poverty there was a third class, made up of yeoman farmers (always a threatened group), rural and urban craftsmen and shopkeepers. Shops in the little towns sold a wide range of goods: many kinds of cloth, haberdashery, whalebone for stiffening clothes and whale oil for lighting, spectacles, tobacco pipes, Bibles and grammar books, gunpowder and pistols, cloves, pepper, ginger, turmeric, fenugreek, prunes, indigo, aniseed, turpentine, and brimstone.

The Welsh economy was largely agrarian, with its chief export the driving of cattle and sheep to the south of England. Grazing, ploughing and charcoal burning severely reduced Welsh woodlands. Wool and cloth were widely produced and sold both locally in fairs and shops, and in England and in mainland Europe. The coal trade, by sea, flourished, as did the manufacture of iron. Silver was a by-product of Cardiganshire mining; in 1637 Thomas Bushell established a mint at Aberystwyth castle which helped pay Charles I's troops in the Civil War. Lead mining also flourished in north-east Wales. Pembrokeshire limestone was quarried and shipped to slake the acid soils of Cardiganshire.

Social rank was in theory rigid, thus securing stability, order, succession; the status quo was an ideal lauded in poetry and prose by English and Welsh alike. Yet everything was mutable. Some people, like younger sons of the gentry, were always at risk of slipping down the social ladder, even into dire poverty, while others struggled to improve their station, and sometimes succeeded. Criminality was rife, murder rates high; men stole animals and killed each other; women stole cloth and clothes, and stifled illegitimate babies. Punishment could be savage, but was frequently mitigated or bypassed altogether.

Wales continued thus through the reign of James I, who succeeded Elizabeth in the loyalty of the Welsh. Even if he did remove the red dragon from the royal arms, was he not still a Tudor by blood? Welshmen remained prominent in court and general affairs. Sir Robert Mansel, veteran of Cadiz in 1596, became Vice-Admiral of England in 1617, a reward for long maritime service. Sir Thomas Button of Glamorgan was made an admiral by James I for his achievements at sea. In 1618 William Vaughan tried to establish a colony, Cambriol, in Newfoundland. Sir John Vaughan of Gelli Aur sailed with Prince Charles to Madrid in 1623 to woo his princess. But in retrospect the most distinguished Welshman of the period was Dr John Davies of Mallwyd (d. 1644), lexicographer, grammarian, anthologist and editor of the 1620 edition of the Bible.

By 1630 Wales was outwardly Anglican, though there were still recusants, while little Independent and Baptist congregations started to appear in the south. But Charles I's endless political follies, especially ruling without Parliament from 1629, caused growing tensions. By 1639 payment of the hated Ship Money tax, by which Charles sought to sustain his rule, was being widely refused.

Civil war between King and Parliament broke out in England in 1642. Wales was divided; the King had many loyal supporters and called on them frequently for men and money, while Parliament too had the backing of some able Welshmen. However, many were willing to turn their coats according to the tide of war and politics, while others retired to cultivate their gardens, hoping to avoid heavy fines and loss of estates.

In England the first Civil War lasted until Charles fled to Scotland in 1646, but dragged on in Wales until Harlech castle surrendered in 1647, the last of many Welsh castles to be besieged. Thousands of Welshmen fought for the king in English battles, and on both sides in Wales and the borders. Strife was particularly fierce in Pembrokeshire, where the Parliament cause was strong. Later in 1647 battle recommenced because the victors could not agree what should happen to the king, nor were their soldiers paid. Parliament's decision to disband the army was badly received, and in 1648 the largest battle in Wales was fought at St Fagan's. Cromwell himself advanced on Pembroke, while royalists in north Wales were defeated in Anglesey. Charles was executed in the following January.

The period 1642–60 was one of the liveliest in modern Welsh history. Philip Jones of Swansea (d. 1674) became one of the most prominent men in government, and survived the Restoration thanks to his tactful dealings. John Jones Maes-y-garnedd, Cromwell's brother-in-law, expected no mercy at the Restoration; he had signed the king's death warrant, and was horribly executed. There was lively religious activity: Morgan Llwyd of Wrexham, poet, writer and Puritan, was prominent in the Fifth Monarchy movement. Vavasor Powell, a prolific writer, was a less amiable personality than Llwyd; he spent most of the last nine years of his life in prison, too turbulent and vociferous to be allowed out for long. John ap John (d. 1694) was the first Welsh disciple of the Quaker George Fox; the two men toured Wales in 1657, making many converts especially in Merionethshire and Montgomeryshire.

For ten years Wales was subjected to a serious attempt to make the country Puritan. The Act for propagating and preaching the Gospel in Wales (1650), administered by a commission under Thomas Harrison, led to the expulsion of many priests from their parishes. Replacing them was more difficult, so itinerant ministers were appointed. Mostly men of principle, they had mixed views on many theological and practical subjects, especially church government and baptism. Education was vigorously promoted, especially by the establishment of sixty free schools, mostly in the eastern counties, paid for out of tithe income.

Despite these reforms, the Commonwealth was not

a success in Wales. There had been too many deaths, too many imprisonments, confiscations and fines. There were strong hints of corrupt administration. Christmas and other popular festivals had been abolished. Church worship was even plainer than that envisaged a century earlier by Edward VI. Social mobility was seen as having gone too far. Economic difficulties rose both from disruption of trade and from coincidental droughts. It is hardly surprising that Wales at large welcomed the Restoration enthusiastically.

Chirk Castle, fiercely besieged in 1659

5. Druids, Methodists, Radicals

The millenial hopes of the Welsh Puritans were crushed by the Restoration; the Anglican gentry were delighted. All was to be, in theory, as it had been before the Civil Wars. Thomas Harrison of the Commission was executed. John Miles, the first Welsh Baptist minister, emigrated from Gower to Massachusetts. Some men regained their confiscated estates, others failed. Religious festivals were restored along with the new Prayer Book of 1662. Tithes were returned to their previous owners, with the result that all the Welsh free schools save Cardigan were closed. Ministers who refused to accept the 1662 Act of Uniformity were expelled from their parishes. They and their followers in their Dissenting churches, whether Baptist, Independent or Presbyterian, were fiercely oppressed. The Quakers suffered most; after 1682 the majority emigrated to Pennsylvania, followed by many Baptists. Five Welsh Catholic priests were horribly executed in 1679, a result of the vile 'Popish Plot' panic. However, the flight of James II and the passing of the Toleration Act of 1689 eased the Dissenters' lot.

The restored Church of England in Wales had some vigour at first. There were several able bishops, mostly Welshmen, and some scholarly, pious and effective

> *The success of the Welsh Bible and the spread of literacy meant that the centre of gravity of Welsh literature moved from poetry to prose; most of that prose was Christian and devotional, and much of it was translated from English. Poetry as a way of making a living had died with Siôn Phylip in 1620, though country poets continued the medieval tradition of praise and 'occasional' verse, without great distinction. Ballads, carols and dramatic interludes were hugely popular. Publication of Welsh books became more frequent once the printing industry was allowed to spread from London. First Shrewsbury, then Carmarthen became important centres for the increasing number of publications.*

priests. But the scene was one of dire poverty among the clergy, while after 1716 no Welshman was consecrated bishop until 1870. Outsider bishops rarely or never visited their sees. Many parish tithes went straight into gentry pockets, with vicars and curates living on pittances, forced to double as schoolmasters, another road to poverty. Church appointments brought Englishmen to parishes where the population was monoglot Welsh. This inevitably helped the spread of Dissent and later Methodism, because the Church was seen as the ally of the gentry and an agent of Englishness.

Dissenters may have been as few as five per cent of the Welsh population of some 300,000, but they were to prove the foundation of what became a slow national revolution in both education and religion. Samuel Jones, expelled vicar of Llangynwyd (d. 1697), made his Brynllywarch home an academy for training dissenting ministers, setting a pattern for higher education in Wales which achieved much success. Dissenters were also given encouragement by an Englishman, Thomas Gouge (d. 1681), who felt called to bring spiritual light to the Welsh. In 1674, aged 69, he formed the Welsh Trust to raise money for schools and for the publication of devotional books in Welsh. His chief Welsh collaborator was the saintly Stephen Hughes (d. 1688), publisher of the work of Rhys Prichard, editor of a new edition of the Bible (1677) and translator of *Pilgrim's Progress* into Welsh. The schools, which seem to have been only partially successful because they used English as their teaching medium, ceased with Gouge's death.

Political life after the Restoration reverted to the old pattern of gentry control. The main purpose of parliamentary membership was to exercise local power and secure government patronage for one's friends and family. At Westminster, Welsh MPs were of small account. After 1688 the cause of the exiled Stuarts was superficially popular, but only one Welsh gentleman, David Morgan, joined the Young Pretender in 1745, and he was executed for his pains. The rest were content to drink his health and keep their estates.

In the Welsh countryside the gentry monopoly was rigidly maintained. While some families used legal devices to prevent the loss of family names and the division of estates among heiresses, others accepted the inevitable. Families like the Vaughans of Trawsgoed, who from the fourteenth century to the present day have produced male heirs in every generation, are rare indeed. Some estates passed into the hands of other Welsh families, many fell to outsiders. Thus, for example, the Wiltshire Talbots acquired the Margam and Penrice estates and the Scottish Campbells gained Stackpole and Golden Grove.

During the eighteenth century the great landowners regularly fell deep into debt thanks to their lavish lifestyles and the number of people they had to support. As a result they had to mortgage their lands. From the middle of the century the wisest began to patronise the new county agricultural societies, seeing that agriculture had to be made profitable, and that productive tenants would pay better and regular rent. There was a bigger market for mineral resources; production of coal, lead and iron increased. Trade, too, was slowly improving; many roads were made better by turnpike trusts, with gentry support, but much depended on the growing number of ships built and crewed by Welshmen all along the British coast. Drovers and their herds left a trail of inns across England – with names such as the

Drovers Arms and the Welsh Harp.

The next effort after the Welsh Trust to raise the level of literacy in Wales was that of the Society for the Propagation of Christian Knowledge, founded in 1699 with strong Welsh connections. Schools were set up and a programme of publishing that lasted for most of the eighteenth century. The schools failed because they

Griffith Jones, Llanddowror

taught in English; the books succeeded because they were in Welsh, including four editions of the Bible of ten thousand copies each.

It was Griffith Jones, vicar of Llanddowror (d. 1761), who revolutionised Welsh education for several generations. He annoyed his bishop with his popular preaching, but was protected by his SPCK patron, Sir John Philipps of Picton (d. 1737), whose sister he married. Jones saw the need to teach monoglot Welsh people through Welsh, and defied anglomaniac critics. The system was simple: Jones trained teachers and the SPCK provided bibles and books, many by Jones himself.

Parishes could invite the establishment of a school if the parish priest was cooperative and a building made available. The scheme mushroomed phenomenally from 1731 onwards, especially among the poor who had no other chance of achieving literacy.

At the same time another revolution was in train. During the 1730s several young men, devoted Anglicans but concerned at the state of their Church, were seized by a new vision. The only ordained priest among them was Daniel Rowland (d. 1790), who, moved by the preaching of Griffith Jones, began to preach with renewed vigour in his curacy at Llangeitho and to travel on mission to his fellow-countrymen. Thus he met Howell Harris (d. 1773), a layman who had begun to preach in 1735 in the open air all over Wales, and who soon won a special convert, William Williams of Pantycelyn (d. 1791), the greatest of Welsh hymnwriters. These men knew the Wesley brothers and George Whitefield, and the name of 'Methodist' soon became attached to them. Harris and Williams were particularly active in establishing Methodist *seiadau* (societies), weekday meetings where members could seek and share spiritual experience. They preferred Whitefield's Calvinistic theology to the milder teaching of the Wesleys, and like the Wesleys, all three Welshmen lived and died as members of the Church of England. Their passionate preaching and exciteable followers drew much criticism.

Thus far, Wales within its borders has been the subject of this book. But there was another Wales developing beyond Offa's Dyke, which is hardly surprising, considering how deeply Wales had been absorbed into England. This was a Wales at once better educated and less religious, living its life in Oxford and London. At Oxford, Edward Lhuyd, the illegitimate Welsh-speaking son of an Oswestry squire, made a considerable name for himself as a botanist and became Keeper of the Ashmolean Museum. He switched his interest to the linguistic and cultural history of Wales, Scotland, Ireland, the Isle of Man, Cornwall and Brittany, and in 1707 published the first volume of his *Archaeologia Britannica*, demonstrating the relationship of the Celtic languages to each other. A series of disasters followed what was an enormous achievement. The book was not well received, though he was elected to the Royal Society. In 1709 Lhuyd died, and most of his enormous collection of unpublished papers was eventually destroyed in two nineteenth-century fires.

More popular than Lhuyd's work were the unscholarly theories of the Breton Abbé Pezron about Celts and Druids, published in 1703 and taken up by Henry Rowlands, author of *Mona Antiqua Restaurata* (1723). Here were the seeds of Druid mania, which provided the Welsh with a new and exciting – if quite fictitious – view of their ancient history and prehistoric relics. At home in Wales, Theophilus Evans mixed an extraordinary cocktail of popular myths in his *Drych y Prif Oesoedd* (1716), much extended in the second edition of 1740 and often reprinted. He clung to the idea that *Cymraeg* (Welsh) derived from the Biblical patriarch Gomer (Gomeraeg = Cymraeg). Meanwhile scholars from Wales, England and continental Europe engaged in lively correspondence about Welsh and Celtic origins.

The foundation in London of the Society of Ancient Britons in 1714 marks the realisation by London exiles of a new way to promote Welsh identity. After the establishment of the successful Welsh School at Clerkenwell in 1738 came the founding of the Honourable Society of Cymmrodorion ('the first inhabitants') in 1751, the Gwyneddigion in 1770, the Druids in 1781 and the Cymreigyddion in 1795, all with close contacts in Wales, keeping alive and reinventing the idea of Welsh identity.

Scholarship of a kind flourished. A heady contribution to Celtomania was the publication of James MacPherson's supposed translations of ancient Gaelic verse, collectively known as *Ossian* (1760, 1761, 1765), which swept Europe in popularity, provoking a remarkable work of scholarship by a poor Welsh curate, Evan Evans (d. 1788). Evans corresponded with leading English scholars interested in Welsh culture, and a wealthy Englishman published Evans's trilingual master-

The Morris circle's antiquarian patriotism can be seen combined with the new Romantic love of picturesque landscape in paintings by the great Welsh artist Richard Wilson (d. 1782) of Welsh castles, especially Dolbadarn and Dinas Brân, and in his pupil Thomas Jones's 'The Last of the Bards'. Taken by the legend that Edward I had ordered the slaughter of the Welsh bards, Thomas Gray had written a fine poem, 'The Bard' (1757). This inspired Jones's painting, which is full of Druido-Celtic symbolism.

Dinas Brân castle

piece, *Some Specimens of the Poetry of the Antient Welsh Bards* (1764). Evans was also part of a revival of the classical modes of Welsh poetry, led by Goronwy Owen and the Morris brothers of Anglesey, Cardiganshire and London, William, Lewis and Richard. The correspondence of these men and their circle is full of delightful gossip and scholarship. They remind us of Shakespeare's Fluellyn – passionately in favour of everything Welsh (except Methodism), capable of savage comment about the English, yet completely loyal to the English crown.

As well as art and music, this eighteenth-century remaking of Welsh culture involved music. While Williams Pantycelyn and many others were composing hymns to be sung to popular tunes, the blind London harpist John Parry (d. 1782) was the first to publish collections of Welsh airs. He was followed by Edward Jones (d. 1824), harpist to the Prince Regent, who published three large volumes of Welsh music and poetry, and by other collectors of Welsh folk-music and dance.

The man who stood on the shoulders of all these scholars and pseudo-scholars was Iolo Morganwg (born Edward Williams, 1747–1826), a list of whose interests is almost endless: poet, propagandist, antiquarian, correspondent, folklorist, memorial sculptor, Unitarian, radical, literary plagiarist, laudanum addict, involved in agriculture, geology, botany, gardening and yet more. He invented a bardic alphabet which he attributed to the Druids, whose descendant he claimed to be, and the *gorsedd* of bards, whose ceremonies continue to attract large crowds at the National Eisteddfod of Wales.

Iolo was one of three editors of an enormous three-volume collection of Welsh literature, *The Myvyrian Archaiology of Wales* (1801–7), providing many texts of genuine medieval literature and some of pure fantasy which Iolo passed off as genuine. Owen Jones ('Owain Myfyr', d. 1841), founder of the Gwyneddigion, financed the venture, while the rest of the work was done by William Owen Pughe (d. 1835), already editor of the poetry of Llywarch Hen and Dafydd ap Gwilym, the latter contaminated by an appendix of Iolo's excellent pastiches. He also produced a huge dictionary of Welsh based on his own eccentric linguistic theories that corrupted a good deal of Welsh usage for the rest of the century.

The Gwyneddigion patronised the revival of the eisteddfod, seeking to change it from being simply a bunch of bards in a back-room bar to a serious poetry competition at Corwen in 1789. Haltingly at first, eisteddfodau in various towns were organised by local societies based on the old Welsh kingdoms: Dyfed, Gwynedd, Powys, Gwent. In 1819 Iolo's Gorsedd was joined to the Carmarthen Eisteddfod.

All this cultural activity was of little interest to the ever-growing Methodist movement in Wales, which remained technically within the Church of England but was increasingly operating on its own. Seven-eighths of the increasing numbers of Welsh publications dealt with religion; the Reformation was finally taking real effect. This thirst for religious works fuelled a growing number of printing presses across the country; they produced biblical concordances and commentaries, sermons, hymns, elegies and fierce disputes between and within denominations. The biggest single project was the 1770 Bible with notes, published in parts by Peter Williams at Carmarthen. The first Bible to be produced in Wales, it was frequently reprinted. All these publications, added to the peripatetic preaching of Methodists and Nonconformists across Wales, did a good deal to tie the Welsh people together across Wales, despite denominational divisions.

Crisis faced Welsh Methodism as the first generation of leaders died. Many members were reluctant to accept communion except at the hands of Anglican priests of whom they approved. Thomas Charles of Bala (d. 1814) was an ordained priest whose Methodism made him unacceptable to the English bishops in Wales. His first great role was as educationist, publishing a famous biblical dictionary, a catechism and a quarterly magazine, and organising an effective network of Sunday Schools. His second was in giving the lead, after years of opposition, to ordaining Methodist ministers who would conduct communion services. The ordinations at Bala and Llandeilo in 1811 marked the founding of a separate body, the Calvinistic Methodist Church of

> *Vividly associated with Thomas Charles is the name of Mary Jones (1784–1864) who, aged 15, walked 26 miles to Bala to buy a Bible from him, carrying her boots lest they be worn out. Charles used her story to inspire the foundation of the British and Foreign Bible Society. Extraordinarily, this genuine Welsh folk heroine does not appear in the Welsh national biographical dictionary or its supplements.*

Wales, the first national institution of modern times in Wales, now retitled the Presbyterian Church of Wales.

Well before the end of the century, other matters were obsessing a handful of Welshmen. While it cannot be claimed that there was a Welsh Enlightenment like that of Scotland, there was a good deal of minor activity of that kind. Books began to appear from 1725 with titles which translate as *A View of the World, A History of the World* and *The Earth and the Firmament* which sought to describe the Newtonian universe. Science lectures were given at the Carmarthen academy. Grammars and dictionaries appeared at intervals, and the other scholarly activities already described can be seen as part of the same movement. So can the influence at the end of the century of the Unitarianism of Joseph Priestley, associated with the radicalism not only of Iolo Morganwg but of the Deist David Williams and the great Welsh philosopher Richard Price, a Freemason. A more orthodox Enlightenment figure is that of Thomas Pennant (d. 1798), gentleman, naturalist, antiquarian and traveller, a great and prolific scholar in many fields.

Radical politics interested a growing number of Welshmen, influenced by Priestley, Voltaire and Tom Paine, and familiar with the English radicals of the 1790s. The most prominent was Jac Glan-y-gors (John Jones, d. 1821) from Cerrigydrudion, pamphleteer and publican. Although his work provoked lively debate and criticism, like the other London Welsh radicals he was never tried or imprisoned, whereas at home the harmless Unitarian Tomos Glyn Cothi (Thomas Evans) was imprisoned in 1803, accused of preaching sedition.

Meanwhile, an even more fundamental change was in train in Wales: the development of serious basic industries. As early as 1723 at Bersham in the northeast, iron was being smelted with coal, not charcoal, and a vigorous industry was born; James Watt's steam-engines used cylinders made at Bersham. A generation later, on the unsympathetic heights of Glamorgan and Monmouthshire, barely fit for raising sheep, the foundations of the first great Welsh contribution to the world economy were being laid. Under the leached soil lay deposits of iron, coal and limestone. At Dowlais in 1748, Hirwaun in 1757, Cyfarthfa in 1765, Blaenavon in 1788, followed by many others, English entrepreneurs could invest the capital that Welshmen lacked or would not venture, building the first major Welsh ironworks. In Anglesey, directed by Welshman Thomas Williams, the equally inhospitable Mynydd Parys was by the 1780s yielding up huge quantities of copper ore for smelting at Swansea or in Lancashire. In Anglesey and Caernarfonshire the little slate quarries were being rapidly enlarged. The exploitation of Wales for its raw materials was seriously under way; the slave plantations of the West Indies provided much of the finance, as in the case of the Penrhyn slate development.

Penrhyn slate quarry

6. Wales Overseas

Welsh contact with the world is sometimes forgotten; we can be too busy defining the national story to be concerned about its apparently random offshoots. Essentially, there are two groups of people involved: those with single tickets and those with returns, i.e. the emigrants and the travellers.

Two forces drive emigration: difficult home circumstances and the promise of a better life elsewhere. Home difficulties mount when people are threatened either by political and religious persecution or by shortage of land and food. Elsewhere might be somewhere else in Wales, or England, or overseas, and the most obvious overseas attraction was America, despite the dangerous voyage. The first important Welsh emigrants were the Baptist followers of John Miles, who left for Massachusetts in 1663. More Baptists followed towards the end of the century, and the Quakers of Merionethshire sailed en masse to the Welsh Tract that William Penn set aside for them in Pennsylvania from 1680 onwards. A St David's Society was begun in Philadelphia in 1729, and in 1730 Welsh books began to be printed in America.

Eighteenth-century migration was desultory until

1794, when the Baptist Morgan John Rhys, supporter of the French Revolution, sailed to the USA, already seen by his fellow radicals as the land of the free. An enemy of slavery and war, Rhys founded the Welsh Emigration Society and bought land in the Allegheny mountains, which he called Cambria, founding the towns of Beulah, now vanished, and Ebensburg. Many Welsh emigrants joined him, men and their families above the lowest level of poverty, who could afford the fares, who wanted more land and desired to escape from the social and economic pressures within Wales. Rhys's aim was to create Welsh colonies which would maintain faith and language in a strange land. One such experiment was attempted in Brazil.

Population growth and land shortage increased the pressure to emigrate during the early nineteenth century. Benjamin Chidlaw, born in Bala in 1811 and taken to Delaware in 1821, returned to Wales on preaching tours and published *Yr American* in 1840, urging people to migrate. Samuel Roberts of Llanbrynmair, the radical Independent minister, pamphleteer, pacifist and anti-slavery crusader, sought to found a colony in Tennessee in 1857, but returned broke and disillusioned in 1867. Another crusader for emigration was Michael D Jones, pioneer of modern Welsh nationalism. He spent three years preaching in Ohio in the 1840s, but realised that Welsh emigrants

Michael D Jones

there were being swiftly acculturated, losing their language within a generation or two – indeed, in the USA the Welsh were considered ideal emigrants for this very reason. Jones's remedy was to establish a colony where there would be no such dangers. He considered Wisconsin, Oregon and Vancouver before turning to Patagonia (see opposite).

Waves of rural emigrants flowed to America from the Caernarfonshire coast, from Merionethshire and Montgomeryshire and particularly from central Cardiganshire into Ohio. Mostly they were tenant farmers who gradually became involved in other economic activities, including the charcoal-iron industry. They built chapels, formed choirs, held eisteddfodau, founded Welsh-language newspapers and published numerous books and several denominational periodicals, in many ways creating the life they would have liked to live in Wales. From Ohio they spread to Wisconsin, Minnesota and beyond.

Another wave followed, of industrial workers – many recruited by American iron, coal and slate companies. David Thomas of Ynysgedwyn was the first to succeed in using anthracite coal to smelt iron, in 1837. By 1839 he had been persuaded to move to Pennsylvania, lured by high wages and first-class travel. The industrial towns of Scranton, Wilkesbarre and Pittsburg held thousands of Welsh industrial emigrants, who were also to be found in Baltimore and the copper, silver and coal mines of California and Colorado. Slate workers migrated to Pennsylvania, New York State and Vermont, while the McKinley tariff crisis of 1890 brought collapse in the Welsh tinplate industry and a last strong wave of migrants. Other Welsh workers helped set up the French steel industry.

From Thomas Jefferson to Frank Lloyd Wright, men and women of Welsh descent have played a part in American history which is beyond the scope of a book like this. They still celebrate St David's Day, research their ancestry, and gather each year in a different city of the USA or Canada in the North American *Cymanfa Ganu*. Migrants to the USA form much the largest percentage of the Welsh overseas, though significant numbers also moved to Canada, Australia and New Zealand.

One related subject that awaits study is that of the migrants who returned to Wales, and indeed the

The legend of Prince Madog's discovery of America in 1170 was just a legend, but it acquired new force during the eighteenth century thanks to Theophilus Evans, and to Iolo Morganwg, who fantasised about establishing a Welsh colony. In 1792 the story sent John Evans across the Atlantic aged 21; over five years he voyaged down the Ohio and up the Mississippi/Missouri to visit the Mandan Indians, Madog's supposed descendants.

surprising number of Americans who came to Wales in the nineteenth century; only the story of the Mormon missions here has been told so far. One temporary migrant was Joseph Parry (d. 1903), the first significant Welsh composer in the classical tradition. Taken to the US aged 9, Parry alternated between America, London

Joseph Parry

and Wales, holding professorships first at Aberystwyth, then Cardiff. His opera *Blodwen* was a huge success, as were his anthems and cantatas, and the splendid hymn-tune 'Aberystwyth'.

What then of the travellers, those who went abroad intending to return? There have been Welsh travellers since the days of the princes who went on crusade to the Holy Land and the pilgrims to Mediterranean shrines. Sir Thomas Button of Glamorgan explored Hudson Bay in 1612–13. Henry Morgan was the most

Sir Henry Morgan

successful of all the Caribbean pirates, capturing Panama City in 1671 and ending as knighted governor of Jamaica. John Evans was in Madras in 1692, diligently acquiring wealth while acting as chaplain for the East India Company, before returning to be bishop of Bangor. Younger sons of gentry sought their fortunes in Barbados and West Africa. In 1776 David Samwell of Nant-glyn sailed with Captain Cook to Hawaii. John Hughes went from Merthyr via Millwall to establish a great ironworks in Russia in 1869; and HM Stanley went to Africa to find David Livingstone in 1871.

For many centuries Welshmen learnt about the world from army service. From Owain Llawgoch and Edward III's archers to Wellington's Welsh generals and footsoldiers, and to the Crimea (where a few might have been nursed by Betsi Cadwaladr); from South Africa via the trenches of the First World War, the Spanish Civil War, the whole spread of the Second World War and subsequent battles in Korea, Malaysia, the Falklands and Iraq, Welshmen fought and died.

From the mid-eighteenth century an increasing number found escape from poverty by going to sea.

It is a cliché, but true nevertheless, that thousands of Welshmen knew the ports of South America and the Far East better than they knew Birmingham or Edinburgh; they even brought home American wives. Ships built in Welsh harbours and creeks traded and were wrecked in all the world's oceans, and their myriad small shareholders, who might never have travelled out of Wales, had an interest in the guano markets of Chile and the wool markets of Australia. Welshmen skippered clippers, tramps and ocean liners, while in the 1930s Potato Jones and Ham-and-Eggs Jones ran their little ships through blockades to succour the Spanish Republicans.

Finally, a small but significant group of Welsh world travellers drew a good deal of attention in the nineteenth century and have left their mark – the Christian missionaries. David Jones and David Griffiths travelled to Madagascar in 1818 and 1823 and worked sacrificially there and in Mauritius. Of other Welsh missionaries worldwide, some active today, the most significant were those who went to the Khasi people in north-eastern India from 1841 until the 1960s. Khasi Christianity and literacy are in considerable part due to this remarkable Welsh effort, still much appreciated by the people. Others went to the South Seas, while Isaiah Brookes Jones went from Colwyn Bay to the Cree people of Canada.

While the Welsh went out to the world, the world kept coming to Wales: Romans, English, Vikings, French, Flemish and Irish. The most colourful incomers to Wales in modern times have formed the maritime communities of the great ports, Swansea, Newport and especially Cardiff, where they were largely concentrated in the now-scattered Tiger Bay community in Butetown. In 1911 some five thousand of Butetown's inhabitants had been born overseas, from China and India to the Yemen, Somalia and the West Indies. Men of fifty nationalities found wives among the local Welsh women. One result of Yemeni immigration from Aden via the coal export trade was the establishment of Britain's first mosque in 1860. After World War II there were Polish communities scattered across rural Wales, with other East European nationalities also present. The Norwegian churches at Cardiff and Swansea represent a long-standing Scandinavian presence in Wales. These communities have provided some of Wales's leading entertainers, boxers, athletes, and a Plaid Cymru Member of the Welsh Assembly.

7. Riot and Respectability

While the Welsh travelled the world, the population at home was rapidly growing; approximately 490,000 in 1780, it was to double within sixty years and quadruple by 1901 to 2,015,000. At the beginning of this period people were fairly evenly distributed across Wales, which was still fundamentally agricultural. But with the explosive growth of iron, tinplate, coal, lead, slate and copper mining, quarrying and smelting there was to be a huge population shift. Eight of the thirteen counties suffered a population decline after 1841, while by 1851 half the people lived in Glamorgan and Monmouthshire. In the north there was movement from the Llŷn peninsula to the quarries, and from the farms to the coal and lead mines and ironworks of the north-east. At the same time there was considerable movement to England as well as migration overseas. The rural population was increasing at a rate the land could not possibly bear; indeed after the peace of 1815, the collapse in food prices caused starvation in some areas. The Cardiganshire countryside resembled the 'congested districts' of Ireland, with beggars everywhere and people boiling grass for soup.

Major engineering works sprouted in the landscape.

Thomas Telford's Menai bridge

Alexander Maddocks sought to develop the Glaslyn estuary as a port (Porthmadog) to replace Holyhead, and created the extraordinary Cob, blocking the tide's access and making the port possible. Welsh canals developed, and at Pontcysyllte Thomas Telford created the most remarkable canal aqueduct ever built. He engineered the road from Shrewsbury to Holyhead, thus destroying Maddocks's dream, with Britain's first suspension bridges at Conwy (1819) and the Menai Straits (1826), designing even the toll cottages himself.

Meanwhile, the ironworks of Glamorgan, Monmouthshire and the north-east were growing in size and number. Men moved from the country to the iron-lands, living as and where they could, their lives a constant struggle against the increasingly dreadful circumstances: more unskilled men than jobs, grim housing, a ghastly lack of sanitation, rampant disease, and a lack of family life for the majority. Work could be in the ironworks, the coal drifts, the quarries or digging the Monmouthshire, Glamorgan, Neath, Swansea and Llangollen canals. Injury meant the end of employment; frequent accidents often caused death. At the same time, and with many of the same difficulties, the mid-Wales cloth trade boomed. The industrialisation of Wales had its fierce drawbacks, not only in accidents and poor conditions, but in the fact that it was too basic; Wales produced iron and coal for others to use in manufacture

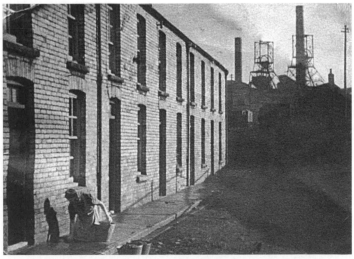

The grim face of Welsh industry

elsewhere. Nevertheless, without these developments, Wales would have suffered the fate of 1840s Ireland. Emigration would not have been a leak, but a flood.

The wars with France were one of the driving forces behind the iron industry's huge success. Ebbw Vale, Nant-y-glo, Beaufort, Rhymney and Aberdare joined the original works on the heights of Blaenau Morgannwg and down the valleys. In the north Bersham and Brymbo flourished. The entrepreneurs – Guest, Crawshay, Homfray, Hall, Bailey, Thompson, Wilkinson – were names to conjure with. They built palatial dwellings for themselves but few did anything for their workmen in the free labour market. Many farmers found it difficult to profit from this potential market because competition was too fierce and their resources miniscule. Meanwhile, landowners complained that squatters were seizing patches on their sheepwalks, while they themselves continued to steal and enclose common land.

The Church of England, totally under the control of government, was unable to create new churches for the growing industrial communities, thus giving a free hand to the chapels. These began to mushroom, providing not only worship but fellowship, education, social ambition and some basic training in democracy, unable however to reach down to the lowest levels of social degradation. At the same time rugged sports flourished – prizefighting, cockfighting and long-distance running. Both rural and industrial Wales were engaged in what seems in retrospect to have been a fierce civil struggle between Riot and Respectability.

A whole range of grievances provoked both rural and industrial disturbances. Harvests were bad, corn prices high and working conditions terrible. Parliamentary reform was absolutely necessary, but vetoed by government. Rents spiralled during the French wars, taxation and tithes were oppressive, tithes being especially obnoxious to the rapidly increasing number of nonconformist farmers. Wages for less skilled workers were always kept to a minimum, and often paid in goods ('truck'). Chronic debt was commonplace. When men and women were driven beyond endurance, sometimes spurred on by local or visiting radical speakers and reading material, rioting was inevitable.

By the 1830s, after a series of problems in both Wales and England, the government was seriously worried about peasant revolt, trade unionism and political activity. From 1793 to 1801 there were corn riots, often led by women; then the struggles of small farmers against enclosure and the squatters against eviction from their *tai unnos* ('one-night houses') endured from 1793 to 1830 and later. In 1816 rising corn prices brought strikes and riots from Amlwch all the way to Newport, exacerbated by wage cuts caused by reduced demand for iron after the end of the Napoleonic wars, and by the presence of soldiers sent to keep order.

For the next twenty years the Scotch Cattle, their name a mystery, challenged the authorities across the Black Domain (western Monmouthshire and parts of east Glamorgan). These men held noisy night meetings, sent threatening letters and handed out beatings in order to sustain strikes, with night visits to blacklegs and agents. Their protests were against all the abuses of pay and commerce perpetrated by industrial owners and their agents. Property was vandalised, tramways broken up and canal barges sunk. A combination of workers' loyalty and terror, coupled with the use of Welsh, made it impossible for the authorities to break the Cattle until 1835, when three men were executed.

Dic Penderyn's grave

In 1831 Merthyr Tydfil caught fire. Serious rioting made the district ungovernable for some days; at least sixteen people were killed by the troops. For the first time a red flag was waved as a symbol of rebellion. Among others the authorities arrested a young man, Richard Lewis (Dic Penderyn), and hanged him for wounding a soldier, though he was certainly innocent; the workers had gained a martyr whose last words ('O Arglwydd, dyma gamwedd' – O Lord, what injustice) are still remembered today. Nor was Merthyr the only cockpit of

David Davies, Llandinam: rail and coal tycoon

trouble; there was unrest among the northern miners, and Carmarthen, a town with a long history of trouble at election time, saw serious disturbances during the election of May 1831.

Despite the hangings, matters did not get better. The failure of the Reform Act of 1832 to offer serious political improvement, the hated 1834 Poor Law reforms, the change in the law by which farmers had to pay their tithes in cash, abuse of the turnpike system (which improved the roads, but at a price) – all these weighed heavily on rural Wales. In the Black Domain orators preached the claims of the Charter, especially its demand for manhood suffrage, to willing ears. In 1839 matters came to a head in both areas. In Pembrokeshire rioters gathered to smash the tollgate at Efail-wen, the opening move of the Rebecca riots. In Gwent five thousand men assembled with clubs and a few guns to march on Newport with the intention of capturing the town and starting an insurrection. Soldiers fired on the marchers, and at least twenty were killed. Eight leaders were condemned to death, but the sentences were commuted; three were transported to Australia, five imprisoned.

Rebecca resurfaced in 1842. Like the Scotch Cattle,

Women played a major part in Welsh culture in the mid-nineteenth century. Lady Charlotte Guest began publishing the Mabinogion *in 1839. Maria Jane Williams published a major collection of folk songs in 1844. Jane Williams, 'Ysgafell', produced her* History of Wales *in 1869. Augusta Hall, Lady Llanover, was a formidable advocate of Welsh language and culture with a particular interest in costume. Sarah Jane Rees, 'Cranogwen', a leading figure in the temperance movement, taught navigation and was the first woman to edit a Welsh periodical.*

men used the old techniques of social disapproval – noise, cross-dressing, face-blacking and terror – ostensibly to destroy the tollgates, more basically to express anger at their circumstances. Like the Cattle, they relied on anonymity, night meetings and the Welsh language to keep enquiry at bay. Troops were sent for, and the newly-founded Glamorgan police force was involved. Late in 1844 the movement lost its violent front, the farmer-participants worried by the increasing involvement of landless men. The sympathy of *The Times* had been recruited; government reformed the turnpike system. It was a rare victory for Riot.

For the rest of the nineteenth century, Riot occasionally raised its alarming head, for example at Mold in 1869, when four people were shot dead by troops after riots provoked in part by an effort by mineowners to prevent the colliers speaking Welsh to each other. However, government had already realised that schoolteachers and policemen would be cheaper than soldiers, but that the voluntary principle could never succeed in the vast field of education without aid. In 1833 the authorities began subsidising the Church and British (i.e. Nonconformist) Societies which had already been founding schools since 1811. Reports were commissioned on the education of the poor in several areas of England and industrial Wales. While in England inspectors commented savagely on rural 'pig-ignorance'

More mighty works of engineering appeared across Wales in the later nineteenth century. Great railway viaducts spanned the valleys, while George Stephenson built the Conwy railway bridge (1849) and the astonishing Britannia bridge across the Menai (1850). Liverpool's huge thirst for water necessitated the creation of the great reservoir at Vyrnwy (completed in 1888 by drowning a village) and the Elan valley reservoirs (opened in 1904 after the deaths of a hundred workmen), supplied Birmingham.

Elan valley reservoir

in Hampshire, Welsh workers were generally praised for their desire for education and the industrialists damned for treating their animals better than their workers. In the meantime county magistrates were reluctantly realising that policemen would be cheaper than soldiers in keeping order. The cause of Temperance began to take hold; there was a slow shift from Riot to Respectability.

All this is background to the iconic publication in 1847 of the 'Blue Books' on the state of education in Wales as a whole. As details of the reports became known, a sea of indignation began to froth which has still not entirely subsided. The three young commissioners were unwisely chosen: all were English, Anglican and without experience. They readily listened to a good deal of evidence from Anglican clergymen annoyed by the success of Nonconformity, and they rashly passed a good deal of adverse comment on social mores for which the people's Nonconformity and Welsh language were blamed. Welsh women's supposed promiscuity was singled out, though illegitimacy was no worse than in England. Anger grew, and was fomented in the Nonconformist press. The ancient 'Treason of the Long Knives', kept in public memory by Theophilus Evans, was invoked, and the occasion was titled 'The Treason of the Blue Books'.

Yet the Blue Books are remarkable not just for their lack of wisdom, but for their accuracy in presenting facts. The vast majority of schools *were* abominably housed, the majority of teachers *were* grotesquely un-qualified. Who else would teach for such dismal wages? Where else but in hovels? The commissioners were impressed by the people's desire for education, especially in English, and the few good schools and the Sunday schools were given glowing reports.

Hitherto, the only higher education establishments in Wales were for training Nonconformist ministers and priests. Now teacher-training colleges were established at Carmarthen, Swansea (for women) and Bangor. Education reformer Hugh Owen drove on the creation of a national university, achieved in a bankrupt hotel in Aberystwyth in 1872. Elementary schooling became compulsory in 1870. All was English medium. By contrast, among the minorities of eastern Europe, long-established compulsory education, although in German, had already created passionate interest in the languages of Slovenia, Estonia and other peoples, leading to their eventual emergence as modern nations. The Welsh by contrast became ever more admiring of English imperialism even as it snubbed them as irrelevant to the modern world and called their language 'the curse of Wales'.

The true obsession of the age (apart from making money) was religion, strong in England, much stronger in Wales. In 1851 a religious census of the two countries was held at government behest. Not surprisingly, despite a host of shortcomings, the results were seized upon. It appeared that while 39% of the English attended worship on the chosen day, 57% of the Welsh did so. Smugness was rampant. Moreover, of the 57%, 80% were Nonconformists, enabling Welsh Nonconformity to turn fiercely on the Church of England. Its bishops were English, its governance unreformed, its finances medieval, reliant on its landholdings not its members; it was perceived as the church of the squire, not the people. Meanwhile chapels were being built at a rate of one every eight days. Gladstone was eventually persuaded to announce that 'the Nonconformists of Wales are the people of Wales'.

Eventually the Church was allowed to begin to reform itself, but another blow fell when the Church of England in Ireland was disestablished in 1869. The Irish situation had long worried Welsh establishment figures. Irish emigrants were arriving in Wales in significant numbers, and there was widespread fear of Catholicism. Suddenly the Welsh Church was vulnerable in the extreme, and attacks began in Parliament.

Twenty years earlier such attacks were inconceivable. Before 1859 every Welsh MP was either a landed squire or an industrialist. The titles of Tory and Whig hardly mattered. Most elections were uncontested; country landowners still regarded their constituencies as theirs by right. However, in Merionethshire in 1859 a Liberal was only narrowly beaten by the Tory squire of Peniarth. Several landlords expelled tenants who had dared to vote against their masters' wishes.

Welsh politics began to burn. The Welsh press was vigorous and influential in both north and south. The Liberation Society, favouring disestablishment of the whole Church, began to campaign in 1862, and Reform Societies were active. Surprisingly it was the realistic Tories who passed the Reform Act of 1867 which increased the number of men able to vote. In the election of 1868 the Whig/Liberals won a majority of Welsh seats, and the result was more victimisation by Tory landlords, an episode which acquired mythical status in Welsh political tradition, and helped secure secret ballots in the future. Several of the Whigs could be defined as Liberals or even as genteel Radicals. The Tories in Wales would never again win a majority. A generation of Liberal politicians emerged who sought improvements in Welsh life: Henry Richard, George Osborne Morgan, Henry Austin Bruce and the unexpected but effective English armaments manufacturer, Stuart Rendel. A second generation followed: Thomas Edward Ellis, D A Thomas and David Lloyd George.

Democracy was on the road even before the county councils were set up. Local boards for health, for the workhouses and for schools all meant that men, and a handful of brave women, could stand for elected member-ship. Women were making progress. Welsh women campaigned for girls' education, against the Conta-gious Diseases Acts,

David Lloyd George

and from 1857 for women's suffrage. In 1870 Frances Morgan (later Hoggan) became the second British woman to graduate in medicine. In 1885 Elizabeth Hughes became principal of the Cambridge Training College for Women Teachers. The Welsh 'mam' of the Valleys acquired mythical status, and cartoonists provided uncouth John Bull with a cringing sidekick, Dame Wales. Women played a prominent part in the Temperance movement, which took such a hold that in 1881 the pubs were closed on Sundays by Act of Parliament – the first Act since 1650 to deal solely with Wales.

Another such Wales-only Act followed in 1889,

creating county education committees to provide intermediate schools largely at public expense, a subject of great Welsh pride since there was no English equivalent. There was however little that was Welsh about the education provided; the use of Welsh even in the playground had often been forbidden even before 1870, and the 'Welsh Not' tag of shame did not disappear until the early twentieth century.

While all these battles were ongoing, Welsh industry was growing and changing. Coal boomed, the Rhondda flooded with immigrant workers, chemical and nickel works polluted the Swansea valley, with anthracite mining and tinplate flourishing to north and west. The iron industry was less dominant; many of the old works had closed, but not before they had supplied rails to many of the new railways being laid in Britain and beyond. Slate production would reach its peak and then begin to suffer competition from cheap tiles. Steam shipping killed off Welsh shipbuilding and the railways the coasting trade.

The railways brought enormous social change to Wales; middle-class women could travel safely, businessmen could get to London and back in a day, preachers moved more swiftly in the age of the train than of the horse. Railways helped the Eisteddfod movement go national in the 1860s. Printing and publishing flourished as never before; paper was cheap, literacy widespread, and wages, though not yet generous, did allow a little extra to spend on books and newspapers. Wales began to produce its own professional and campaigning journalists, of whom Thomas Gee of Denbigh was the greatest, and a major publisher to boot.

In the 1880s further Acts of Parliament brought extended suffrage, and rang the death-knell of Welsh landowner power with the

Thomas Gee

foundation of the County Councils in 1889. Only in Breconshire did Tory squires and their followers gain much success; elsewhere the Liberals swept them away. Taxation and agricultural depression began to force them to sell their estates.

There were signs everywhere of a renewed Welsh self-awareness. People began to give their children Welsh names. Choirs sprang up, especially – but not only – in the valleys, their feats in Wales, England and the USA avidly followed. Another myth was born, not without justification: Wales as the Land of Song. But while the Welsh were gaining national confidence, it was cultural and industrial rather than political. Attempts by Ellis

> *Welsh creative effort was boundless, in art, in music (characteristically in minor keys), but above all in writing. Poets produced vast reams of verse in both strict and free metres, virtually all of it now unreadable. Prose however achieved greatness in the novels of Daniel Owen and the prophetic journalism of Emrys ap Iwan, both men able to stand back and cast a cool eye on the weaknesses of Welsh society, religion and politics. A patriotic song by two innkeepers of Pontypridd, Evan and James James,* Hen Wlad Fy Nhadau, *eventually became the Welsh national anthem. It was later borrowed by the Bretons.*

and Lloyd George to promote a Welsh political agenda, however moderate they seem now, were premature.

Nevertheless, in the south the days of the Liberals were numbered. Unionism, so long the bane of government and capitalists, was getting organised. In 1886 the South Wales Miners' Federation sent Mabon (William Abraham) to Parliament. He gained credit with the miners by winning them a monthly day's holiday, and from the coalowners by negotatiating a sliding scale of wages. Mabon's political allegiance, so to speak, was Liberal/Labour, although there was no Labour party as such. An attractive character, hugely popular as an Eisteddfod leader, Mabon lost influence after the refounding of the Miners' Federation in 1898. He could not prevent the slide into a series of viciously contested miners' disputes led by syndicalists and socialists, embattled against mineowners inevitably concerned above all for their profits. The election of the Independent Socialist Keir Hardie for Merthyr in 1900 was followed by the rise of the Labour Party to a century of power in Wales.

Ever since the 1650 Act for propagating the Gospel in Wales, the country has had its own history of education. The establishment of the national University with widespread popular support stimulated the passing by a Conservative government of the Liberal-inspired Welsh Intermediate Education Act of 1889. This made secondary education available across the country in advance of England, administered by county committees. The Central Welsh Board (C.W.B.) was set up in 1896 to coordinate and administer the system, including examinations. Sectarian difficulties remained, inspiring the 'Welsh Revolt' against the consequences of the Education Act of 1902, but compromises were engineered. Welsh authorities were far more generous with grammar school provision than in England, and led the way, starting with Anglesey, in establishing comprehensive schools. For several generations Wales produced a surplus of trained teachers who found a welcome in English schools. In 1948 the C.W.B. became the Welsh Joint Education Committee, owned by the 22 local authorities.

8. The Worst and Best of Times

In 1900 Wales was facing in all directions at once. Coal was so successful that labour flowed in from England, Ireland and beyond. Cardiff had grown from a village to an international centre of enterprise in shipping and coal exports; Swansea was a world centre for metallurgy and chemicals, Llanelli for tinplate. Welsh businessmen flourished both in Wales and in London, Liverpool and Manchester. Association and rugby football had gained a firm grasp on the male population. Boxing flourished too; in 1914 Freddie Welsh became world lightweight champion, the first of a line of Welsh world boxing champions. There were now three colleges in the national University: Aberystwyth, Cardiff and Bangor. Swansea would join in 1920.

In fact the omens were not good. The countryside was still bleeding its Welsh-speaking population; the influx from elsewhere was rapidly eroding the language in the south-east. True, the number of Welsh-speakers was increasing, but not as fast as the population, which had reached two million. The slate industry was in crisis, facing a three-year strike, and the railways became an industrial battleground. The growing suffragette

> *Although the Church had solved most of its problems, the Nonconformist establishment ('the Liberal Party at prayer') was still set on Disestablishment, despite vigorous opposition in Wales and beyond. Meanwhile the Roman Catholic church grew apace; in England it gained a Welsh leader, Cardinal Vaughan (d. 1903) and in Wales an archbishop of Cardiff in 1916.*

movement in Wales continued to struggle against fierce prejudice.

However, a series of events boosted morale. There was the Revival of 1904, which drew world attention and boosted the chapels, and though it proved to be a straw fire, it became part of the national myth. Cardiff was given city status in 1905. The victory of the Welsh rugby XV over the All Blacks at Cardiff Arms Park

The National Museum, Cardiff

The National Library, Aberystwyth

became a legend; meantime soccer fans delighted in the
genius of Billy Meredith. The replacement of Tory by
Liberal government in 1905 was followed by the Liberals' election landslide of 1906, which swept the Tories
from every Welsh constituency. Lloyd George brought
in the first old age pensions. The National Museum and
National Library of Wales were given royal charters in
1907, with fine buildings to follow. Cardiff, now the
largest town in Wales, began to look like a capital city
with a splendid Civic Centre. Lloyd George took time
from the great People's Budget and the muzzling of the
House of Lords to engineer the 1911 investiture of the
Prince of Wales at Caernarfon. In the same year John
Edward Lloyd published his monumental *History of
Wales*; for the first time Welsh history was an academic

discipline. In 1914 Church leaders bowed to the inevitable and a Disestablishment Act was passed; for the first time there would be an archbishop of Wales. Surely all was well.

Not so. British industry had started to lag behind its great competitors, Germany and the U.S.A. World shipping was turning from Welsh coal to foreign oil, and house-roofing from Welsh slates to cheaper English tiles. Welsh industry relied on supplying raw materials; factories hardly existed. Welsh industrial housing was still shocking; infant mortality terrible. Tuberculosis killed in the countryside and the valleys alike. Industrial unrest grew. Coalminers were influenced by a new generation of anarcho-syndicalists for whom both capitalism and nationalisation were unacceptable. The 1910 riots at Tonypandy became a working-class legend, with the Home Secretary Winston Churchill inaccurately accused of using troops against the rioters, though the only death was not at military hands. Matters were actually worse at Llanelli in 1911, when troops opened fire, killing several people. A long series of coalmine disasters culminated in 1913 with 439 deaths at Senghennydd. There were anti-Jewish and anti-Chinese riots.

Suddenly Britain and France were at war with Germany, taking most people completely by surprise. Nor was it fully realised, in spite of European and American precedents, that armaments had become so

Cardiff City Hall

efficient that enormous slaughter would follow; protest was stifled by respectable conformity. Nonconformity was divided; a few ministers became virtual recruiting officers, a few became principled pacifists (George M Ll Davies, Tom Nefyn) while the majority wrung their ineffective hands.

Ordinary Welshmen volunteered and were later conscripted en masse – 272,000 of them. Bellowed at and cursed in demotic English, they learnt to wield bayonets and fire machine-guns, only to stumble through mud and barbed wire to trench foot, gas, disillusion and death. Thirty-five thousand died; thousands more were blinded, crippled or traumatised. At home the miners saw the chance to better their pay; unrest was only stifled by a government takeover of the coal industry in 1921. The regiment of Welsh Guards was founded in 1915 as a gesture to the Welsh feeling to which Lloyd George so readily appealed, disingenuously claiming (with Belgium's shattered neutrality in mind) that this was a war on behalf of the little nations. The war's martyr in Welsh memory was the poet Hedd Wyn (Ellis Evans) of Trawsfynydd, who was awarded the Chair at the Birkenhead National Eisteddfod of 1917 five weeks after his death at Pilkem Ridge, the bardic chair swathed in black.

Women were deeply involved in the war. Apart from the loss of husbands, fathers, brothers, sons and fiancés, they gained invaluable if shattering experience as nurses, drivers, or working in munitions, the Post Office and the Land Army. This brought them the vote in 1918, though the soldiers' return meant a forced retreat to hearth and kitchen. However there was now a small but significant female graduate population, involved most commonly in teaching, so long as they did not offend local councillors by marrying.

After the 1918 election the

Hedd Wyn

wartime coalition became essentially a Conservative government with Lloyd George, Prime Minister since 1916, in the chair. His main contributions to Welsh life at that time were to secure the continued building of the National Library, and to rescue the nascent Church in Wales from the worst of the financial retribution threatened in 1914. The post-war Liberal collapse affected Wales: from 35 MPs in 1906, only 10 were elected in 1929, while from 1924 onwards the Labour party never had fewer than twenty.

If the war had been an earthquake in Welsh life, another was to follow. The industrial crisis was slow to develop, and did not affect the seaboard of north and south as it so terribly did the valleys and mining towns. Coal export markets declined. There were lockouts and military patrols. The coalowners, themselves threatened by market conditions, reduced wages until a general strike was called in 1926 in sympathy with the miners. Its collapse after nine days left the miners on their own, and from 1930 onward, with a decline in the steel market, the Welsh valleys were destitute. Women starved themselves into ill-health trying to keep their menfolk and children going. The government even considered abandoning Merthyr altogether in favour of a new coastal settlement. The Prince of Wales famously said that something should be done, but little was, save the establishment of a new steelworks in Ebbw Vale and the Trefforest Trading Estate. Communism thrived, and 400,000 people, many of them Welsh-speakers, left Wales for England and beyond. It was the biggest catastrophe in Welsh history; the population was virtually the same in 1951 as it had been in 1921.

The disaster affected the Welsh language. In 1901, 929,824 registered themselves as Welsh-speakers, effectively 50% of the population. In 1911 the figure was even higher at 977,824. Then absolute decline set in, especially after 1931; by 1951 the figure was 714,686, reflecting the exodus of the 1930s. Moreover the decline was especially obvious among younger people. There were two institutional reactions to what some perceived was the decline of Welsh national life. One was the establishment in 1923 of *Urdd Gobaith Cymru* (the Welsh League of Youth), a non-political youth language movement, founded by Ifan ab Owen Edwards. The other came with the establishment by a small group of the Welsh Nationalist Party at Pwllheli in 1925.

In 1936 a gesture of an entirely new nature was made on behalf of the Welsh language.

Dancing at an Urdd Eisteddfod

D J Williams, Lewis Valentine,
and Saunders Lewis

Alarmed by German militarism, the government needed to establish a bombing school. Foiled by protestors at sites in England, they turned to Pen-y-berth on the Llŷn peninsula. Enraged by this, several members of the Welsh Nationalist Party staged a fire at the site and then surrendered to the police. Saunders Lewis, university lecturer and literary critic, the Reverend Lewis Valentine, Baptist minister, and D J Williams, teacher of English at Fishguard, were put on trial. The Caernarfon jury could not reach a verdict, and an alarmed government illegally transferred the trial to the Old Bailey, where they were sentenced to prison. Afterwards Valentine returned to his congregation and Williams to his school (teaching Welsh, not English!), but the

If national life seemed to some to be in decline, Welsh literature and scholarship flourished. New poets had come on the scene from 1900 onward: T Gwynn Jones, Robert Williams Parry, T H Parry-Williams. Kate Roberts mastered the short story. Welsh scholarship became a full-time occupation for a handful of scholars working in the little Welsh departments of the University of Wales; Ifor Williams in particular made available the greatest Welsh medieval texts. Saunders Lewis, himself a poet and later dramatist, virtually invented Welsh literary criticism. A major pool of English writing was created by Welshmen: Caradoc Evans, Rhys Davies, Lewis Jones, and later on Glyn Jones, Dylan Thomas, Vernon Watkins and Idris Davies.

Kate Roberts

University College at Swansea, said to be under pressure from industrialists, sacked Saunders Lewis. Ironically the bombing school never functioned thanks to frequent mists, but a legend had been born. In the eyes of a minority, illegal action had been given currency.

The wholly expected 1939 return of war brought more suffering and drama to Welsh life. Thousands of

The fortune accumulated by David Davies from his railway, coal and harbour ventures enabled his grand-daughters, Margaret and Gwendoline Davies, to turn their home at Gregynog into an extraordinary oasis of the arts between the wars. They made a wonderful collection of French art, now in the National Museum, and established the Gregynog Press to produce fine printing and bindings. There was a regular music festival supported by Sir Walford Davies, Gustav Holst and other distinguished musicians. Classical music in 20th-century Wales was led by two women, Morfydd Llwyn Owen and Grace Williams, and by Daniel Jones, Alan Hoddinott and William Matthias (d. 1992). Englishwoman Winifred Coombe Tennant supported Welsh-born artists in difficult times.

evacuated schoolchildren arrived in the rural north and west, disrupting schools. Both men and women were conscripted for the armed forces, the mines, munitions and land work. Invasion via Ireland was feared and precautions taken. Agriculture, which had been dreadfully depressed after the Great War, was revived by the government, knowing that a U-boat blockade could starve Britain into surrender. Tons of blackberries and rosehips were picked by schoolchildren for jam and syrup, lorryloads of rabbit corpses ferried to English cities. In 1941 the Luftwaffe blitz hit Swansea, Cardiff and Deeside, killing a thousand people. The tiny Welsh Nationalist Party barely survived the war, and then only thanks to the efforts of the Oxford-educated son of a Barry shopkeeper, Gwynfor Evans. The core membership of the party were pacifists, some on grounds of Christian conscience, a few arguing that while Wales lacked its own government they could not participate in the war. It seemed unlikely that the party would have any serious role in the country's future.

At the war's end hundreds of Polish exiles settled in the Welsh countryside, adding to the country's ethnic mix of valley Italians and Spaniards. Cardiff's Tiger Bay, where immigrants from Africa and beyond had long settled and intermarried happily with Welsh girls, was often cited as a model interracial community despite its poverty, but Cardiff's planners eventually wiped it out.

With the Labour landslide of 1945 Welsh politicians were back in the position Lloyd George had enjoyed from 1906. Real reform was needed, and was now possible. Farming was not allowed to collapse into ruin as it had been after the First World War. James (Jim) Griffiths secured a new deal for National Insurance and for disabled workers, while Aneurin (Nye) Bevan triumphantly initiated the National Health Service, foreshadowed in the wartime Beveridge Report. They represented two shades of Welsh Labour: Griffiths the Welsh-speaker from the anthracite coalfield, Bevan the flamboyant radical orator, with little time for the Welsh

In 1957 Parliament authorised Liverpool to drown the Tryweryn valley to improve their already adequate water supply, ousting the inhabitants of Capel Celyn. No Welsh MP voted in favour The work was disrupted by acts of violence in 1962–63 by young men inspired by the Pen-y-berth action. This was followed by some years of attacks on English-owned holiday housing in the Welsh-speaking heartland, which had public support from the greatest of recent Welsh poets, the Rev. R S Thomas. Tryweryn symbolised the powerlessness of political Wales. Liverpool City Council apologised for its arrogance in 2005.

language or home rule ambitions. Lloyd George, Griffiths and Bevan were the Welsh makers of the British welfare state.

Labour lost the 1951 General Election despite winning 200,000 more votes than the Conservatives Britain-wide. The latter offered Wales the sop of a part-time minister. The Home Secretary Sir David Maxwell-Fyfe ('Dai Bananas') would represent Wales in Churchill's cabinet, the real work being done by a junior minister. Cardiff was officially made capital of Wales in 1955, and the city staged the Empire Games in 1958.

All this while London governments had found it difficult, even threatening, to cope with Wales as a unit. True, Wales had its own Board of Health and

Education Department, but the nationalised coal, steel, water, railway, gas and electricity mostly divided Wales between north and south (that ancient curse) or lumped parts of it with English regions. The 1948 Council for Wales was both secretive and toothless: as was said at the time, 'It exists because Wales is a nation: it is not given any power in case Wales behaves as a nation.' With Labour's return to power in 1964 the promise of a Secretary of State for Wales was realised with the appointment of Jim Griffiths and the creation of a Welsh Office in London and Cardiff, bearing a wide range of responsibilities. This not only created a Welsh Civil Service career structure, it was the turning-point after which it became easier to ensure the establishment of national bodies such as the Wales T.U.C. and the Conservatives' creation of a separate National Curriculum for schools in Wales.

Change had already begun in Welsh schools. Worried by the threat of evacuees, Ifan ab Owen Edwards had established a private Welsh-medium primary school at Aberystwyth in 1939. In 1948, Carmarthenshire established the first state primary school for Welsh-speakers in Llanelli. A remarkable Director of Education, Haydn Williams, initiated a vigorous language policy in Flintshire schools, establishing the first Welsh-medium secondary school at Rhyl (now at St Asaph) in 1955. Others were opened in Denbighshire and Glamorgan,

A Cymdeithas yr Iaith protest

later spreading to the west and back north. By 2001 the impact of the schools was clear in the census figures, especially for the south-east, which showed an increase in the number of young Welsh-speakers.

Whether in or out of London office, Labour had its usual majority of Welsh seats and iron control of the most populous county councils, Glamorgan and Monmouthshire. The height of parliamentary supremacy was reached in the General Election of 1966, when Labour held 32 seats, the Conservatives three and the Liberals one. But politics was changing. In 1962, Saunders Lewis gave a powerful St David's Day radio address, appealing in effect for serious protest on behalf of the

Welsh language against its miserably subservient status. In response a group of young men and women formed *Cymdeithas yr Iaith Gymraeg* (the Welsh Language Society), which over the next decades led a remarkable campaign. Members protested against English road-signs by painting them out. They conducted sit-ins in post offices and government institutions. They refused to register their babies in English. Dafydd Iwan's popular ballads gave them further heart, and when he was sent to prison, he was visited there by the Archbishop of Wales, Glyn Simon. Plaid Cymru began to gain serious votes in by-elections.

Place-names began to change: Caernarvon and Llanelly became Caernarfon and Llanelli. Others

Gwynfor Evans, Dafydd Iwan: campaign for Welsh-language TV

brought out their traditional Welsh names, often heard but rarely seen, and put them on bilingual signs. The language movement went from strength to strength; it was an early sympton of the international awakening of a generation of youth no longer in awe of its elders. Nor was it simply the young who were moved to change; *Merched y Wawr*, the Welsh-language alternative to the Women's Institutes, was founded and spread rapidly across the country. So did Welsh *papurau bro* (community newspapers), made possible by cheap printing. The Welsh Books Council, begun on a minute budget by the remarkable Cardiganshire librarian Alun Edwards, grew steadily. On the other hand chapel congregations were shrinking rapidly and buildings closed at a startling rate.

Social conditions improved, slowly at first. Many

Gwynfor Evans

council housing estates were built in both towns and countryside; some flourished, some developed severe social problems. By the end of the 1960s electricity had reached every village and most farms, and television along with it. Central heating became common, with complex social effects on family and society alike. By the 1970s cars were common, making long-distance shopping easier and starting to kill village shops, a task carried on by the multiplication of supermarkets.

Labour's triumph of spring 1966 was suddenly dented by the extraordinary Carmarthen by-election four months later. Gwynfor Evans, who had stood in every election since 1945, brought off the most sensational victory in twentieth-century Welsh politics. The government responded by moving the Royal Mint to Llantrisant, establishing the D.V.L.A. at Swansea to mop up unemployment and by committing to the investiture of the Prince of Wales at Caernarfon in 1969, after he had spent a term at Aberystwyth learning Welsh.

Children's graves at Aberfan

> *The Welsh valleys had had to live with mountainous slagheaps smearing the landscape until 21st October 1966, when a huge tip fell on Aberfan, killing 116 children in their primary school and 28 adults, all drowned or crushed in a flood of slurry. Even in European terms it was a unique catastrophe, spawned by past capitalist greed and gross contemporary official negligence, for which no-one was punished. As a result a great many slagheaps have now been cleared to prevent any such disaster in the future.*

Meanwhile, the Welsh landscape was deeply marked by change. Large tracts of mountain land were planted with conifers. Mixed farming and hay meadows disappeared; grazing livestock and silage spread everywhere, making much of the countryside a green desert but profiting farmers. Council estates, begun after WWI, dramatically increased after 1945. Three National Parks were created. Nuclear power stations were opened at Trawsfynydd (1965) and Wylfa, Anglesey (1971), while numerous railway lines closed. The first Severn bridge was opened in 1965, launching Wales's first motorway across the south, and a second bridge was begun in 1996. Terraced houses in the valleys had their slates replaced by tiles. Rural and urban chapels were converted to other uses, fell into ruin or were demolished. Urban centres were 'redeveloped' leaving Swansea,

Newport and Bridgend almost soulless. Welsh castles were cleaned up and promoted for the tourism that is now Wales's biggest industry. Farms were amalgamated, farmhouses sold off and land rented out.

Employment in Wales was traumatised. The coal industry which once employed 250,000 men had collapsed to one tenth of that figure by 1981. The miners' successful strike of 1973 gave some union leaders the impression that they could stop pit closures and even bring down a government. But the election of 1979 brought in the Thatcher government, determined never to be thus humiliated again. In 1983, a strike was ordered without a national vote or proper planning, with disastrous results for the miners of Wales. North Wales was left without a single pit, the south with several opencast workings, the Big Pit museum at Blaenafon and Tower Colliery, Hirwaun, sold to a successful miners' cooperative but eventually closed. The marvellous Workers' Institutes of the valleys became bingo halls or shut down altogether.

Wales had been at the heart of British steel production in the 1960s, with giant works at Port Talbot, Llanwern, Ebbw Vale and Shotton. But global change meant that while production grew more efficient, competition was fierce and the workforce shrank with the closure of Ebbw Vale, Shotton and Llanwern. In the three years from 1979 Wales lost 130,000 jobs overall.

The southern ports shrivelled in size and importance; marinas grew.

Of course there were industrial success stories. The oil industry based on Milford Haven flourished for a while, but without a great access of employment. Car engine manufacture at Bridgend was also successful. Japanese electronics companies came, and some went. Service industries and government employment grew. Entry to the European Community in 1973 brought benefits: better roads, cleaner seas and support for agriculture.

Welsh sporting achievements were too manifold to list, but mention must be made of pre-war Cardiff's F.A. Cup win, of Glamorgan cricket's two championships, of many rugby Triple Crowns, of successes in snooker, of Lynn Davies's 1966 long-jump Olympic medal, of soccer's John Charles and Ryan Giggs, of the inimitable Tanni Grey-Thompson and of Wales's first black international champion athlete, Colin Jackson. Among performers, pride was boosted by great actors, Richard Burton, Siân Phillips and Anthony Hopkins, and especially by the world-class Welsh National Opera company with which the greatest Welsh singers, including Geraint Evans and Bryn Terfel, have sung. The B.B.C. has made a national symphony orchestra not only possible but successful. Welsh popular singers flourished: Shirley Bassey, Tom Jones and Cerys Matthews.

Bryn Terfel

Most national institutions did well: the National
Museum gave birth to the splendid Museum of Welsh
Life at St Fagans, the Slate and Wool Museums at
Llanberis and Drefach Felindre, and the National
Maritime Museum at Swansea, as well as Big Pit. The
National Library developed political, sound and visual
archives; the National Eisteddfod became a flourish-
ing behemoth; Llangollen's International Eisteddfod
brings performers from all over the world. Welsh art
galleries, few in number, began to give room to major
Welsh artists. Only the University of Wales lost its way
as a national body: in 2007 the federal structure was

replaced by a confederation of independent institutions, while the largest body, Cardiff, left the structure altogether. The University is still responsible for the University Press, the Dictionary of the Welsh Language, the Gregynog Conference Centre and the Centre for Advanced Welsh and Celtic Studies at Aberystwyth.

The story of change is not only endless but accelerating. Welsh local government was completely revamped not once but twice, both times by Conservative governments. The eight large counties constructed in 1974, with historic Welsh names, were replaced two decades later by 22 unitary authorities, giving Wales a structure rather different from that of England. The revival of national feeling brought three Plaid Cymru MPs to parliament in 1974 and gave the party some success on county councils. The Wilson government published a report on devolution, and the Callaghan government held a referendum on home rule in 1979, only for it to be utterly rejected. There was a general fear of letting go of nurse for fear of finding something worse.

Perhaps this failure of will led the Thatcher government to believe that they could break their 1979 Queen's Speech promise to create a Welsh-language television channel. Hitherto Welsh television had been a muddle; the B.B.C. could only broadcast in Welsh at unpopular hours, commercial TV was divided between two companies, while an attempt to create a Welsh

The Rt. Hon. Carwyn Jones,
First Minister of the Welsh Assembly Government

commercial company had failed. Welsh Language
Society members had campaigned for years for a
separate TV channel. Gwynfor Evans responded to the
government's U-turn by announcing that he would
go on hunger strike to death. Persuaded by Welsh
leaders that Wales would become ungovernable if that
happened, the government backtracked and in 1982,
S4C began broadcasting. A Welsh media industry was
created, giving employment to hundreds of talented
people who otherwise would have left Wales. Meanwhile, Welsh-language Acts passed by the Conservatives
gave the language better status, effectively removing it
from the political agenda. Bilingual supermarket signs,

so long governmentally abhorred, proved unobjectionable everywhere.

The Conservatives' last gift to Wales was the bizarre appointment of the right-wing ideologue John Redwood as Secretary of State for Wales. On top of all the industrial damage done after 1979, this helped ensure that when in 1997 the Blair government offered Wales another devolution vote, it squeaked through by a tiny margin, thanks in no small measure to the leadership of Ron Davies and Dafydd Wigley for Labour and Plaid Cymru respectively, with strong Liberal backing. The Assembly elections were held in 1999, and though Ron Davies's career sadly imploded, Rhodri Morgan provided two terms of sane and sometimes witty leadership. He was succeeded in 2009 by Carwyn Jones. Pioneer reforms, often followed by London, have been initiated: the Children's Commissioner, a Commissioner for the elderly, free bus transport for seniors, a ban on smoking in public areas and free medical prescriptions.

The 1997 devolution vote was surely Wales's last chance for constitutional growth. The steady flow of retired people from England into the Welsh countryside, often driving house-prices beyond local reach and transforming local speech, is bringing about a peaceful form of ethnic and cultural replacement, especially along the coast and in what has been *Y Fro Gymraeg*, the Welsh heartland. Today it is not Gwynedd or the south-west which has the largest percentage of Welsh-born people but the old industrial area of the valleys. It is true that, thanks to S4C, BBC Radio Cymru, Welsh-medium education, the Welsh Books Council, the Welsh-language Acts and Welsh-language Google, those who choose to do so can live their lives largely in Welsh. Yet they are only a minority even among the 20% who speak Welsh. S4C in 2010 faces a difficult future. Of the industries which employed Welsh-speakers in large numbers – coal, tinplate, slate, agriculture – only agriculture barely survives. Teaching and tourism are not sufficient replacements. The chapels, once the heart of Welsh-language culture, are largely moribund, and while the Church in Wales has provided the Church of

The Senedd building in Cardiff Bay,
home of the Welsh Assembly Government

England with its first Welsh archbishop of Canterbury, Rowan Williams, its authority in Wales is not what it was. The Welsh press – i.e. the *Daily Post* and *Western Mail* struggle valiantly against the tide of London papers.

After the 2007 Assembly elections the political parties had trouble coping with the idea of coalition. Wales certainly faces serious problems: the shrunken manufacturing base and over-reliance on public employment; the declining birthrate; impossible house prices, and continuing poor health. However, with the aid of European grants and the block grant from London, Wales can to some extent make its own way in the world, including no doubt making its own mistakes. The Assembly's handicap is that it has wide administrative responsibility, where mistakes easily draw criticism, but limited regulatory power. But its very existence is a source of some astonishment to those of us with long memories, for it has created its own evolving political and legal culture. More powers will certainly be delegated to the government of Wales, whether or not there is a plebiscite in the future for giving the Assembly legislative powers. Wales has gone through many reinventions, but there seems no end yet to its ingenuity.

Further Reading

There is a huge amount of material relating to Welsh history which can be tracked from the works listed below. Most are in print at the time of writing and are available at reasonable prices.

General
John Davies, *A History of Wales* (Penguin, 2007)
Geraint H Jenkins, *Concise History of Wales* (Cambridge, 2007)
G E Jones & D Smith, *The People of Wales* (Llandysul, 1999)
J Graham Jones, *A Pocket Guide: the History of Wales* (Cardiff, 1990)
Prys Morgan (ed.), *The Tempus History of Wales* (Tempus, 2005)

Early and Medieval
A D Carr, *Medieval Wales* (MacMillan, 1995)
R R Davies, *The Age of Conquest* (Oxford, 2000)
R R Davies, *The Revolt of Owain Glyn Dŵr* (Oxford, 1995)
Wendy Davies, *Wales in the Early Middle Ages* (Leicester, 1981)
Gerald of Wales, *The Journey through Wales & the Description of Wales* (Penguin, 1978)

M Green & R Howells, *A Pocket Guide: Celtic Wales* (Cardiff, 2000)

Frances Lynch & others, *Prehistoric Wales* (Sutton, 2000)

Kari Maund, *The Welsh Kings* (Tempus, 2000)

Mark Redknap, *Vikings in Wales* (Cardiff, 2000)

W H Manning, *Roman Wales* (Cardiff, 2001)

Roger Turvey, *The Welsh Princes* (Longman, 2002)

Glanmor Williams, *Renewal and Reformation in Wales c. 1415–1642* (Oxford, 1993)

Early Modern and Modern

R Davies, *Hope and Heartbreak: A Social History of Wales 1776–1871* (Cardiff, 2005)

D Gareth Evans, *A History of Wales 1815–1906* (Cardiff, 1989)

D Gareth Evans, *A History of Wales 1906–2000* (Cardiff, 2000)

G H Jenkins, *The Foundations of Modern Wales: Wales 1642–1789* (Oxford, 1993)

K O Morgan, *Rebirth of a Nation: A History of Modern Wales* (Oxford, 1998)

G Dyfnallt Owen, *Elizabethan Wales: The Social Scene* (Cardiff, 1986)

Glanmor Williams, *Wales and the Reformation* (Cardiff, 1999)

T M Charles-Edwards & R J W Evans, *Wales and the Wider World* (Shaun Tyas, 2010).

Also by Gerald Morgan

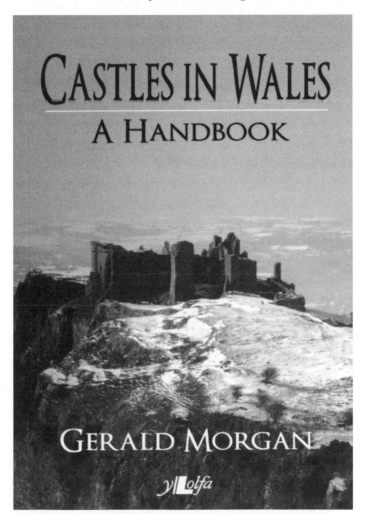

Castles in Wales
A Handbook

Gerald Morgan

y Lolfa

£4.95

A Brief History of Wales is just one
of a whole range of Welsh interest
publications from Y Lolfa. For a full list
of books currently in print, send now for
your free copy of our new, full-colour
Catalogue – or simply surf into our
website, **www.ylolfa.com**, for secure,
on-line ordering.

Talybont, Ceredigion, Cymru SY24 5HE
e-bost ylolfa@ylolfa.com
gwefan www.ylolfa.com
ffôn (01970) 832 304
ffacs 832 782